GRANDMA
KNOWS
Best

GRANDMA
KNOWS
Best

Practical advice that
has stood the test of time

JANE MAPLE

ARCTURUS

This book is intended as an informal guide to life, health and household. While every effort has been made to ensure this book contains warnings, where necessary, about the possible dangers of substances mentioned herein, it may be advisable to consult a qualified medical practitioner before use. The publisher, the editor and their respective employees shall not accept responsibility for injury, loss or damage occasioned to any person acting or refraining from action as a result of material in this book, whether or not such injury, loss or damage is in any way due to negligent act or omission on the part of the publisher, editor or employees.

ARCTURUS

This edition published in 2010 by Arcturus Publishing Limited
26/27 Bickels Yard, 151–153 Bermondsey Street,
London SE1 3HA

ISBN: 978-1-84837-748-6
AD001676EN

Printed in China

Contents

Introduction

I love being a grandma. Even though I don't feel aged – in my mind I'm still in my 30s, and I'm lucky enough to have kept myself sprightly in my old age – my years on this planet have left me with a canny wisdom and some wonderful memories that I love to share with those younger than myself. And I would love to share them with you.

While I do my best to understand the modern world, I often yearn for the simplicity of the years gone by, where we made do with what we had and didn't worry if our neighbour had a more up-to-date wireless or some trendy new shoes. If we could afford it we bought it; if we couldn't we simply went without.

I look at the changes happening today and the pressures people put themselves under to compete and I have to shake my head. Sometimes I think the world has gone mad, losing sight of the lessons by which we lived our lives when I was a girl. My grandchildren look at the past and wonder how we got by without computers, mobile phones and goodness knows what else, but life was simpler then and I couldn't have been happier.

So I'm asking you to take a step off the treadmill, slow down and take time to enjoy some of the things I used to take for granted. I like to think I have worked out ways of coping with most situations that life throws at me and am long enough in the tooth not to be taken in by the traps of the modern world.

My childhood was a whirl of imaginative play, free from the reliance on new-fangled contraptions that children today take for granted. We created our own entertainment. Some of my fondest memories are the times spent with my grandma, a remarkable person whose spirit was undiminished by her advancing years. She was astute, wise and above all a lady. 'Good old fresh air and some imagination is all you need,' she used to say.

We would sit round the fire once the sun had gone down and she would read us one of our favourite stories. She taught me how to knit, to crochet, to sew. She taught me how to milk a cow, collect eggs from her chickens and tend a small vegetable patch. If my trousers were torn or badly worn, she mended them. If I had a sore throat, she made me honey and lemon.

My grandma believed that children should do their fair share of work around the house and I remember standing on a three-legged milking stool so that I could cross off my job for the day on the chart that hung from the parlour door. If I wanted a new toy, I either had to go to grandpa and beg and plead with him to make me one – he was a dab hand with wood – or get grandma to knit me something from scraps of wool that had been unravelled from worn-out old jumpers.

I hope you'll take heed of these 'old-fashioned' ideas. They're as relevant today as they ever were. They've served me well, as they did my mother and grandmother and countless generations before them. I'm sure they'll stand you in equally good stead.

Grandparents bestow upon their grandchildren
The strength and wisdom that time
And experience have given them

A Word
of Advice

Lessons From The Past

Take a deep breath and make-believe you are on a journey into the middle of last century. It's hard to imagine, I know: there are none of the luxuries we take for granted today, but then again none of the temptations to lead us astray. Not so many, anyway! My grandma was clever at saving the pennies. She would ask for the offcuts at the butcher's, or the slightly bruised fruit and veg that had been put at the back of the greengrocer's shop. If she had been particularly frugal on a day's shopping, then I was allowed to go into the local sweetshop and buy a penny's worth of liquorice. I still consider that a special treat.

I believe that if you can get your children to appreciate the simple things in life and not have everything that Johnny Down the Road has got, then they will start to value what they do have and will take more pleasure from them.

Please don't think I was an angelic child – I can assure you I had my moments. I vividly remember pestering both my grandparents and my parents to be allowed a puppy. I don't remember how long I cajoled and pleaded with them to come round to my way of thinking, but my grandma finally came up with a solution. She said if I was prepared to save threepence a week from my pocket money to buy a collar, a lead and a bowl, then she would take me down to the farm to choose a puppy when the next litter was born. At last I could see that my dream would come true, provided I fulfilled my side of the bargain. I was absolutely thrilled.

Money Sense

Money has become – or perhaps I should say has always been – a major part of our lives. If we do not learn to manage our money properly it can be a real cause of stress, and stress is a killer. At the very least it can leave us feeling run down and unable to function to the best of our ability.

'Look after the pennies and the pounds will look after themselves,' we were always told. It might be a dusty old proverb, but it is one that is well worth repeating. Money sense doesn't always come naturally and it is something you might need to be taught. Some people are too proud when it comes to money. Don't be afraid to ask for help. But take my advice and try to live within your means. There is nothing worse for the mind and body than going through life with debts and worrying about paying them back.

There is a wonderful lesson in money sense in the story *David Copperfield* by Charles Dickens. David lodges with a family called the Micawbers, who live in abject poverty. The Micawbers are constantly plagued by their creditors and, even though the family does nothing to help themselves, they truly believe their situation will change for the better. Change it does, but for the worse, and the Micawbers are sent to a debtors' prison while the little they own is taken from them. It brings to mind the old proverb, 'A fool and his money are soon parted'. So don't be a fool, watch your pennies, and remember, every penny saved is a penny earned.

KEEP TRACK OF YOUR MONEY

To avoid the fate of the Micawbers, the easiest way to keep on top of your spending is to buy yourself a little notebook. If you don't want to go to the expense of buying one that is ruled specifically for financial transactions, just a simple lined notebook will do the job adequately. Now write down all your outgoings for the week so that you will get a sense of reality about exactly what you are spending. It is easiest to start with your regular outgoings such as rent or mortgage, utility bills, shopping and travel. Then write down every single transaction you make that week. If, when you add all your expenses up at the end of the week, you find you are spending more than you are earning, then try to think of ways you can make some savings. For example, did you really need that new lipstick or that piece of steak for dinner on Friday? Use the example on the opposite page as a rough guide for recording expenditure.

Although you might find this a little difficult to do at first, I can assure you that you will quickly get into the habit of writing everything down. I still do it and if I have a few pounds left over at the end of the week, well, I put these by for a rainy day! I can hear you saying now, 'What does that mean?' Well, I don't care who you are, there will always be that occasion when you need a little extra cash. For example, if the washing machine has flooded the kitchen and you need to call out a plumber. Or you might have to take an unexpected trip to the dentist, or the dog to the vet – all things that are not part of your weekly budget.

ENCOURAGE YOUR YOUNGSTERS TO SAVE

While on the subject of putting money by, I used to encourage my children to save some of their pocket money each week.

29

January (Week One)

	MONEY IN	MONEY OUT
Wages		
Family allowance		
Rent/mortgage		
Council tax		
Electricity		
Gas		
Telephone and internet		
Water rates		
Mobile phone		
TV licence		
Car insurance and tax		
Petrol		
Food		
Eating out		
New shoes for Johnny		
Sundries		
Totals		

This is not only a great way of teaching them the value of money but I believe it is character-building too. I bought both my children and grandchildren piggy banks to keep in their bedroom so they could see just how much money they were managing to put by.

My grandson recently asked me, 'Nanny, why do we keep money in pigs and not, say, dogs or cats?'

A really good question, I thought, but one that I couldn't
answer immediately.

'Would you give me a little time to answer that one, please?'
I asked him.

He gave me an old-fashioned look and simply replied, 'But I
thought you knew the answer to everything, Nanny.'

I laughed and replied, 'Oh, if only I did, I would own
the world!'

Anyway I did look into the origin of the piggy bank and
thought I would like to share this little piece of knowledge with
you (see opposite).

My children occasionally asked if they could borrow money
when their allowance had run out. My response to that was
always, 'Neither a lender or a borrower be,' and in that way
you could stay out of trouble. I tried to get it into their heads
that they simply couldn't have what they couldn't afford – after
all, I had to save for everything I wanted as a child. A harsh
lesson maybe, but it has stood them in good stead ever since.
Occasionally I had tears because they didn't think my ways
were fair, but they soon learned the valuable lesson – after all
if wishes were horses, then beggars would ride!

Finally, another piece of advice I would like to impart is
to encourage your children to work for their pocket money.
There is nothing wrong with asking your kids to help around
the house, walk the dog, wash the car or help sweep up the
leaves in the garden. Quite simply, they will value things that
they have worked hard to earn. That's how I was brought up.
For each job I completed I received a point and for each point I
received a coin. I learned the value of money quickly and nine
out of ten times spent it wisely.

WHY IS IT CALLED A PIGGY BANK?

So why exactly do we save our coins in a piggy bank? Pigs aren't really hoarders like, say, squirrels, who hide their nuts away to get them through the winter. The answer is that in a way it was a mistake or a misunderstanding of the word 'pig'. During the Middle Ages (around about the 15th century) metal was too expensive to be used on household wares, so pots were made out of an orange-coloured clay called 'pygg'. The clay pots were used to store many items such as salt, flour and possibly coins as an early form of saving.

In the early 19th century, allegedly, an English potter was asked to make a 'pygg bank' which he misunderstood as 'pig bank' and produced a savings jar in the shape of a pig. This pig, of course, became very appealing to children and the custom of saving money in a pig has stuck ever since. Many European countries believe it brings good luck to give a piggy bank as a gift. Also many major banks and building societies have adopted the idea of a piggy bank, hoping that it will encourage children to save their pennies.

THE DANGER OF CREDIT CARDS

My considered opinion of credit cards is not to have one at all. I know this sounds harsh, but the danger with these little pieces of plastic is that you can buy expensive items without realizing that you are actually spending money. My advice would be that unless you are able to pay the total off each month when the statement comes through the post, then don't take the risk of running up debts. These debts will only mount up because the credit card companies love nothing more than you owing them money so they can charge some extortionate interest rate. In other words, don't bite off more than you can chew.

If you know you can afford to keep on top of the payments, that is well and good, but I still feel it is better to save for the item you would like as you will then be far more appreciative of your new possession. It will also make you think very carefully before buying. Take everything into consideration and be honest with yourself whether you really want the new coat or posh pair of boots or whether it's just a passing whim.

SHOPPING WITH CARE

With escalating prices and such a wide choice of food to buy, it makes sense to plan ahead by making a shopping list before setting foot inside a supermarket. If you carefully select the items you really need, you will be able to do your weekly shop without making too much of a dent in your purse. Here are a few useful pointers:

* The first items to go on your list should be the basics such as milk, bread, eggs and cheese. Check your refrigerator first to see whether you really need any of these things.
* Always look for items that have been reduced. You can save a lot of money this way, although you might find you have to use them up a little faster.
* Check the prices. You might find quite a difference between the various brands.
* It is usually economical to buy larger sizes of items such as washing powder.

* Cut out coupons from papers for things you normally buy and carry them with you in your purse.
* Take advantage of loyalty cards as these can give you a nice little windfall every couple of months.
* If you are worried about how much you are spending, carry a pocket calculator with you and punch in each item as you put it in your basket.

If you are shopping for personal items such as cosmetics, clothes or shoes, try to avoid distractions. The longer you linger in a shop and start browsing, the more tempting it will be for you to spend money on things that you don't really need. Just remember, you can't have your cake and eat it, at least not all the time. Appreciation of what you have leads to greater satisfaction and if you take a leaf out of my book you can learn to be happy with very little.

A Question of Etiquette

Can anybody explain to me why etiquette is no longer considered important? As a child I always made sure to mind my Ps and Qs. If I forgot to say please or thank you, my parents would tell me a fairy had been locked in a cupboard and wouldn't be allowed out until I remembered.

You might feel such values are out of date and have no part to play in modern society. I say poppycock! *Manners maketh man.* Every society on Earth has its own set of manners and impoliteness still creates ill-feeling today just as much as it did when I was a girl. Some people seem to think they're too busy or too important to bother with such niceties, but good manners cost nothing, as the saying goes. They can help to make those around you feel comfortable, and there is no greater compliment than knowing people want to be in your company.

Good manners start at home so, this is where the lessons have to begin. Anyone who says it isn't necessary for children to say please if they want something is talking rot. I would say to my children and grandchildren alike, 'Haven't you forgotten a little word?' This used to make them stop and think and it wasn't long before please and thank you became a nice habit of theirs.

Another bone of contention in my book of manners is snatching. I remember my daughter being in tears at a birthday party because her friend had simply snatched the present out of her hand without having the good manners to say thank you. This was when I realized that my lessons had sunk in.

TABLE MANNERS

Children can only learn by example and my table manners were learned from sitting down with the family for meals at the weekends when we were all together. Too often these days busy schedules do not allow families to eat at the same time, but it is worth making the effort to sit down together at least one day each week, even if only for Sunday lunch. This can give your child valuable lessons on how to behave at the table. Grandma always said, 'Children should be seen and not heard,' and she would never allow us to be loud at the table or talk with our mouths full. If these manners are learned at home, then you will always be able to take your children out for meals, whether it is at someone else's house or a restaurant, without feeling embarrassed by their behaviour. This goes for adults too.

DO'S AND DON'TS AT THE TABLE

* *At the start of the meal, unfold your napkin and place it on your lap.*
* *Hold your knife and fork with the handles in the palm of your hand. Put your forefinger on top and your thumb underneath.*
* *When you have finished eating, place your knife and fork side by side in the middle of the plate.*
* *If you are unable to finish your food, it is acceptable to leave some on the side of the plate.*
* *Ask politely if you need to leave the table before the end of the meal.*
* *Do not eat with your elbows on the table.*
* *Always make a point of thanking your host.*

LAYING THE TABLE FOR A DINNER PARTY

The idea of laying a table properly for a dinner party is not
to intimidate your guests, but to help put them at their ease.
All your guests need to remember is to start from the outside
and work their way inwards when it comes to using cutlery.
I always think that if a table is laid properly it says a lot about
the host.

* The traditional choice of tablecloth is white, but any plain
  colour will suffice as long as it is fairly pale and not boldly
  patterned.
* If you want a centrepiece make sure it is no higher than 15 in
  (38 cm) so it will not obstruct the people sitting opposite you.
* Now position the dinner plate approximately 1 in (2.5 cm)
  from the edge of the table, leaving 2 ft (61 cm) between each
  person to allow adequate elbow room.
* Use either linen or cloth napkins and place them in the centre
  of the plate. See opposite for an attractive way to fold them.
* The golden rule for using cutlery is to work from the outside
  in. The knives are always to the right of the plate and the
  forks to the left. A soup spoon, if required, should be placed
  on the right outside the knife. Dessert cutlery should always
  be placed above the plate with the fork facing right and the
  spoon positioned above this with the bowl facing left.
* Depending on how many different wines you intend to serve,
  the glasses should be positioned above the knives. A water
  glass should be to the extreme left and then follow in the
  order for which they will be used, working from left to right.
* The side plate should be positioned to the left of the forks
  with a butter knife laid across it.

THE CROWN NAPKIN

This napkin fold might take a little practice, but it is well worth the effort to make your guests feel like royalty. It helps if the napkin is starched to stop it sagging in the middle. Remember, practice makes perfect.

1. Fold the napkin in half diagonally. Turn the napkin until the open ends are pointing away from you.

2. Fold the right corner up so that its point is resting directly on top of the middle corner. The edge of this new flap should lie directly on the centre line of the napkin.

3. Repeat the last step on the other side to create a diamond shape. Fold the bottom of the napkin up about one third of the way up and press the fold down well.

4. Curl the left and right sides of the napkin so that they meet in the middle. Then tuck one into the other.

5. Now stand the napkin upright and pull at it where needed so that the shape is symmetrical.

6. The finished crown napkin.

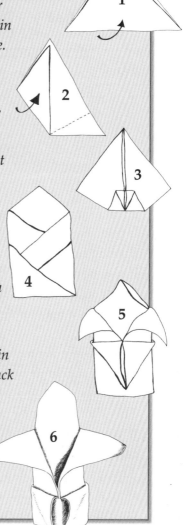

ETIQUETTE IN THE OFFICE

Although it has been 'several' years since I have worked in an office, I still believe that in today's competitive world where jobs are not so easy to come by, social etiquette can go a long way in making you a popular workmate. Above my work station I always used to have in large letters – 'NEVER PUT OFF UNTIL TOMORROW WHAT YOU CAN DO TODAY' – which was something I managed to adhere to most of my working life. I tried to be pleasant even when in a bad mood and quickly learned to bite my tongue rather than say what was on my mind. I have tried to update these snippets of wisdom for the modern workplace. They still hold good.

* Try to keep your desk tidy and definitely do not spread your clutter into someone else's work space.
* If you share an office, always ask before opening a window or turning on the air-conditioning.
* If you borrow anything from one of your colleagues, make sure you return it to its rightful owner.
* If there is a tea/coffee rota, make sure you know when it is your turn.
* Make sure your mobile phone is either turned off or on 'silent', and limit personal calls to a minimum.
* Don't spend your work time looking at personal websites. This should only be done in your own time.
* If you are allowed to eat at your desk, try to avoid sandwiches or foods that have a strong smell.
* Always be polite when speaking to someone on the phone, even if they are testing your patience. Remember – the customer is always right!

Natural beauty

Natural beauty is all about loving the body and face we were born with. With age, what we consider to be natural beauty starts to fade and gravity starts to play its part. Everyone, big or small, fat or thin, is beautiful in their own way, but it is how we perceive ourselves that really matters. We can use make-up and other clever tricks to enhance our beauty, but I am afraid nothing can take the place of wholesome living and a nutritious diet to keep our bodies running at full capacity. If purse strings are tight, or you feel some of the more popular beauty treatments are overpriced, why not try some of my tried and trusted cleansers, exfoliators and moisturizers, which have both a refreshing and detoxifying effect. But remember, whatever route you choose to take, inner beauty shines most brightly.

* *Buttermilk, yogurt and cream all make excellent cleansers for the skin, giving it a natural glow. They also help to plump up the skin, giving it a younger appearance.*
* *Use almond oil after a bath or shower to keep your skin soft and supple. This oil also speeds the healing process and minimizes the risk of scarring.*
* *Make a simple exfoliator treatment by mixing sugar and water. Simply soak your face with a warm flannel for a few minutes before applying the solution and gently massage your skin before rinsing off.*

The main aim of this part of the book is to get you to feel good about yourself and not to go craving a look that just isn't you. Just as an example, don't try to emulate some of the models you see in women's magazines. Just picture in your mind's eye what they look like first thing in the morning before they hide behind a veil of make-up. I have learned over the years to be happy with who I am – sunspots and all – and now appreciate that I am loved for who I am, not what I look like. It is a difficult pedestal to reach, but it is a great feeling when you get there.

You might be one of those lucky people who have normal skin. If you are, then you should be able to achieve its natural radiance by drinking plenty of water, eating a balanced diet and taking regular exercise. Remember a lot of dry skin problems can be caused by dehydration, so it is important to moisturize yourself from within as well.

Eating nuts can also help if you have dry skin, because they contain many beneficial oils which can help keep your skin supple. Do not use very hot water when bathing or showering if you have dry skin.

I have included some tips on both dry and oily skin which, with regular use, can make a considerable difference. Oily skin tends to be more prone to eruptions, so try to keep it squeaky clean and avoid touching your face as much as possible. Of course, there are advantages to having oily skin: it does not lose its elasticity so quickly, which means it stays looking younger for longer. Can't be bad, eh? And that's without any botox!

Just a quick warning: before you try any of the remedies mentioned in this book, perform a patch test to make sure you do not suffer any bad reactions.

OILY SKIN

❋ *Aloe vera gel is great at absorbing oil and clearing out the pores. Dab the gel on to your face two or three times a day and then allow it to dry.*

❋ *Milk is an excellent oil-free cleanser. To get rid of make-up residues left on the skin, mix 2–3 drops of sandalwood or lavender oil with 2 tablespoons of milk and massage gently all over the face.*

❋ *Oily skin benefits from being moisturized and honey can give it a healthy glow without making it feel greasy. Apply a thin layer all over the face, then wash it off with tepid water after about 15 minutes.*

DRY SKIN

❋ *Massage the face and body with almond oil or olive oil every night before going to bed.*

❋ *Mash a ripe banana and apply it to the face and neck. Relax and leave on the skin for about 15 minutes before rinsing with warm water.*

❋ *Make a mixture of 1 egg yolk, 1 tsp of orange juice, 1 tsp of rose water and a few drops of lime juice. Apply to the face just before you get in the bath and leave on for 15 minutes before rinsing off with warm water.*

❋ *Aloe vera is soothing, healing and moisturizing and also helps to remove dead skin cells.*

EAT YOUR WAY TO NATURAL BEAUTY

If you find you are always struggling
to maintain that natural, healthy look,
you might like to rethink your diet and
pastimes. Vitamins, minerals and nutrients
are all essential for cell renewal and it is
these new cells that provide your skin with that
natural, healthy glow. Try these few simple steps to change the
way you eat and consequently enhance your natural beauty.

* *Try to cut down on the amount of fatty foods you consume. Protein is the building block to a healthy body, so increase your intake of both animal and vegetable protein. Did you know that the pea is packed full of both vitamins and proteins and also essential fibre? Why not grow some in your back garden? Eaten regularly, they will help give you a radiant complexion.*

* *There's a lot of truth in the saying, 'an apple a day keeps the doctor away'. They are full of vitamin C and also a vital fibre called pectin. Pectin helps promote the growth of strong nails and hair.*

* *Include oily fish, such as salmon, mackerel and herring, in your diet at least twice a week. Oily fish are rich in Omega-3, an essential fatty acid which helps to fight inflammation within the body.*

* *Drink plenty of fruit juice, especially citrus juices, as they are rich in antioxidants.*

* *Exercise daily. Walking, swimming or cycling on a regular basis will keep your body fit, young and healthy.*

THE IMPORTANCE OF EXFOLIATING

I don't think I realized the importance of exfoliating until I holidayed in Turkey. As a treat after a long train journey I decided to go for a Turkish bath. After getting over the shock of being treated like a piece of meat being prepared for the barbecue, I actually enjoyed the experience. The first part of the procedure involved a rather large woman throwing buckets of warm water over me and then rubbing my whole body quite vigorously with a rough mitten. I was totally amazed at the amount of dead skin that came away, and even more amazed at how good my skin looked for the next couple of weeks.

New skin is regenerated every day and natural exfoliating can help to remove the dead cells which can stop the new cells from forming and block the pores. It also helps to stimulate blood circulation, which can stand you in good stead when you reach my ripe old age. Here are some exfoliating blends that you can try at home:

* *It is essential to exfoliate oily skin. Use a gentle scrub of 1 tablespoon of rice powder mixed with 1 tablespoon of cornflour and a few drops of lemon juice.*
* *Beauty salons often use sea salt as a natural exfoliator. Firstly apply some olive oil all over your body and then massage your skin with sea salt. Make sure the granules are not too large – if necessary put them through a grinder first. After exfoliating, rinse your skin with warm water and apply some baby oil to rehydrate.*
* *If you have sensitive skin, a mixture of honey and oats works as an abrasive to remove impurities from the skin.*

Creating a Cottage Garden

My cottage garden is not only a place of tranquillity but also provides me with many of the plants I use for medicines, food, fragrance and also making natural dyes. The secret is to choose the right plants and combine them with some rustic charm. Quaint little brick paths, climbing plants over home-made trellises and perhaps a fish pond with a few goldfish and waterlilies help to complete the scene. There are plenty of picture postcards depicting beautiful cottage gardens, and they are not nearly so hard to recreate as you might think. I am going to give you some simple steps to help get you started. In a traditional cottage garden, plants are grown very close together in a seemingly random fashion. Although it looks as though little planning has gone into the planting, this is not the case: it takes very careful forethought to make it all look so natural.

I have utilized every inch of space and my patio is surrounded by beautiful stone pots filled with every imaginable herb and whatever flower is in season. Remember to leave one small space for a seat so that you have somewhere to escape to when the hustle and bustle of daily life gets too much for you. There is nothing more relaxing than sitting in a beautiful garden, listening to the birds and smelling all the different scents around you, with a glass of something soothing in your hand.

Once you have got your soil in good condition

by digging it and adding plenty of well-rotted compost, the fun part is choosing the plants. If you are unsure about what plants to grow in your type of soil, then either read gardening books, ask an expert at your local garden centre or pick a friend's brains. When planning your flowerbeds make sure you plant the tallest plants at the back, gradually decreasing in height to the front where you can put some small fillers. This way one plant will not detract from another's beauty.

Originally cottage gardeners did not have a lot of money to spend on plants, so they would save seeds from the previous season, dry them and have a fresh supply for the next season. You could leave part of your garden wild like a meadow and just encourage wild flowers to grow there, such as primroses, cowslips, bluebells and daisies, to name but a few. To enhance this area, you could have a rustic piece of garden furniture made out of recycled materials. Old chimney pots, earthenware drainage pipes and even old tyres planted with flowers can

---

HOW TO GROW A CHAMOMILE LAWN

The easiest way to start a chamomile lawn is to grow it from seed. You will need to start these in seed trays and when the seedlings reach a reasonable size you can plant them out 4 in (10 cm) apart. When the plants reach approximately 6 in (15 cm) in height, trim the lawn to encourage growth. Once established, the chamomile lawn seldom needs cutting and is beautifully fragrant. Make sure you keep the lawn watered during dry spells. You might find a chamomile lawn difficult to grow if you live somewhere with clay soil as they prefer a light, sandy base.

make a really attractive addition to a cottage garden. I have one area to the side of my cottage that has a beautiful chamomile lawn, which not only cuts down on the amount of mowing I have to do (as does the wild meadow), but also provides a beautiful scent on a warm day.

If you want to grow climbing plants such as honeysuckle, clematis, rambling roses or wysteria, then a pergola or arbour can make a wonderful feature. Several different climbers can share the same support, and it is a great way to add colour and scent at a different level, especially over a seating area or as an entrance to your garden.

Cottage gardens also look good if they are broken up by a path: shingle, crazy paving or red brick can be really attractive. Traditionally, cottage paths were straight and a mixture of earth and cinders, but be imaginative with yours and make them windy or curved to give your garden even more character. Here are some tips to make your cottage garden extra-special:

* Try to create a relaxed and informal atmosphere. You can add to this by making sure you have plenty of scented plants so that the garden is full of heady aromas. Rosemary, lavender, roses, jasmine and honeysuckle are all beautifully scented.
* Concentrate on colours that go well together. In my garden I have certain spots that I have designated for one colour. It works really well to see various shades of white as your eyes focuses on all the different heights.
* Remember, no cottage garden is complete without roses.
* Use structures such as pergolas and arches to break up the different sections.
* Above all, enjoy the peace and serenity that you have created

Finally, in this section I would like to give you some tips on how to encourage wildlife into your garden. All animals are vital to the ecosystem and not only will they be beneficial to the upkeep of your garden, they are also a delight to watch. I always encourage my grandchildren to sit quietly and draw what they see.

There are plenty of small things you can do to adapt your garden without disrupting its natural beauty. The basic requirements for any animal are food and shelter, so here are some simple suggestions to attract wildlife.

* A pond is the best single thing you can add to your garden to attract wildlife. This will encourage birds, insects, mammals and amphibians to your garden. Make sure your pond has gently sloping sides to allow things to climb in and out, as well as deeper areas and also some stones to allow animals to sit and absorb the sunlight. You can make your pond look really pretty by including aquatic plants such as water lilies.
* Hedgerows and shrubs provide perfect shelter for many animals and also encourage birds to build nests. Try to include some evergreen shrubs or hedges in your garden to provide all-year-round protection against the elements.
* Compost heaps are great for attracting all kinds of insects, slow worms and very often a hedgehog will choose to hibernate in the warmth of the rotting matter.
* Rockeries and dry stone walls can give shelter to frogs, toads and newts as they are attracted by the damp, dark area beneath the stones.

❋ It is a good idea to leave some old logs lying in a corner of the garden as the rotting wood makes a perfect habitat for all kinds of insects and invertebrates. My children were absolutely fascinated the first time they saw a stag beetle with its amazing 'horns'.

❋ Make sure you plant plenty of flowers that are rich in nectar to encourage bees, butterflies and moths. These include: monkshood, bugle, foxglove, hollyhocks, anemones, aubretia, borage, campanula, wallflowers, poppies, geraniums, gypsophila, sunflowers, hellebores, bluebells, candytuft, honeysuckle, poached egg plant, honesty, forget-me-not, rhododendrons, clover, verbena and zinnia.

❋ During the cold winter months, birds look for extra food to supplement their diet. You can help them out by putting a bird table in your garden and giving them scraps from your kitchen along with peanuts and other types of birdseed. This should encourage the birds to stay in your garden even when the weather gets warmer.

❋ Place some nesting boxes in secluded places in your garden to encourage birds to breed. Think what a joy it will be for your children to see the baby birds as they start to brave the big wide world. You can even buy nest boxes which are specifically designed to attract bats.

Perhaps one of the most important things about attracting wildlife into your garden is to avoid using any type of chemical intended to control pests. Although you may get rid of the unwanted pest, these chemicals can have a harmful effect on the beneficial wildlife too. Try to find natural ways of dealing with pests that will not harm the environment or our animal friends.

Fresh Air, Fun and Frolics

Now that you have created this beautiful, peaceful haven, I want you and your family to make full use of this outdoor space. I want to encourage families to make the most of being in the fresh air, even if the weather is a little temperamental. I remember sitting in a small wigwam I had made for my grandson out of a few garden canes and an old bedsheet last summer. We were just about to have our first mouthful of jam sandwich when I heard rain drops on the roof of the tent. I peered out and said, 'Oh dear, it's raining cats and dogs!' My grandson looked aghast at me and quickly replied, 'Nanny, won't they break our tent as they fall?' I laughed until tears rolled down my cheeks, and so did my grandson after I explained it was just a silly expression that grandma used.

HOW TO ERECT A SIMPLE WIGWAM

Get eight garden canes and push the ends into the ground until you have formed a circle. Gently push the tops of the canes together at the top and tie together using some string. Tie securely. Get an old sheet or tablecloth, cut a small hole in the centre and place over the cane structure so that the tied part at the top is poking out of the hole. Next take some clothes pegs and peg the bottom of the sheet to the base of each cane to stop the sheet being blown away. Now take a pair of scisscors and cut a slit in one side and peg both sides back. Leave the rest to your child's imagination.

HOPSCOTCH

In one corner of my garden I laid a set of paving stones in such a way that my grandchildren could play hopscotch and I also let them write on the stones with chalk without being scolded. None of their friends knew the game, so it was fun to take them to the bottom of the garden and teach them how grandma used to play. For those of you who do not know how to play, here is a brief description.

* Using a piece of chalk mark out ten squares as shown in the diagram on the right.
* Each player uses a marker such as a stone, a shell or even a beanbag.
* The first player stands in front of the number 1 square and has to throw her marker into the square without it touching any of the edges. Then she hops over square 1 and lands with one foot in square 2 and one in square 3. She continues, putting only one foot in each square in order. On reaching square 10, she turns round and hops back, pausing in square 2 to pick up the marker, then hopping into square 1.
* The game is continued by the player throwing her marker into square 2 and continuing as before, always hopping over the square that contains the marker.
* The player is out if the marker fails to land in the proper square, or if she treads on a line or loses balance when bending over to pick up the marker.

Hopscotch can be played by any number of players, girls or boys, taking turns.

A TREEHOUSE

Dear old 'Grumps', as grandpa is affectionately known, built a tree house for our grandchildren. He erected it by making a basic wooden platform around a tree trunk with a ladder up one side and a slide to get down the other. He made a wall by attaching sides from an old shed which he cleverly adapted to fit. He made a kind of thatched roof out of old branches, which he tied together using raffia to make it look natural. Kids can have hours of fun turning it into a fort or a pirate's cave. It is out of bounds to adults, which makes it even more special – although I have been known to join in the odd adventure from time to time, with permission from the kids of course!

BARBECUES

Barbecues are always a wonderful way to make use of the garden and a great way to get the whole family together. You can either buy a traditional barbecue or build one of your own out of household bricks. These fit in perfectly with your cottage garden, are inexpensive and very easy to make.

TREASURE HUNTS

Another way of getting children into the garden is to organize a treasure hunt, or a chocolate egg hunt at Easter. I hide the gifts the night before and then make up a set of clues to help the children find the treasure. It can last for quite a while with older children, especially if the clues are a little cryptic. This has always been a great source of amusement for my family. Make your treasure hunt themed and, as an alternative to written clues, you can make a drawing and then cut it into pieces so that the children have to fit it together just like a jigsaw.

REMEDIES FOR ALL THE FAMILY

Laughter is the Best Medicine

I was always taught that 'an ounce of prevention is worth a pound of cure' and I still believe that, even in today's world of advanced medical know-how, it still holds true. After all, it is far better to prevent a medical problem than to have to face up to the stress of trying to cure one. In my heart, old-fashioned though it may be, I truly believe that laughter is the best medicine you can have. It works wonders, especially if you are going through a particularly tricky period in your life. How often have you smiled when you hear a child laugh? Hard not to smile, isn't it, because laughter is so infectious?

Try to remember the last time you had a really good laugh – not just a chuckle, but a real good belly laugh. Can you remember how good you felt afterwards even if it made your stomach muscles ache at the time? There is a medical reason behind this: laughter induces physical changes within your body that lead to a greater feeling of wellbeing. Laughter triggers the production of chemicals called endorphins, which are what give us a feeling of happiness. Laughter is also a powerful medicine because it strengthens your immune system, boosts your energy levels, lessens pain and protects you from the damaging effects of constant stress. Most of all, like all the best things in life, it is free!

There is nothing that can work faster or more effectively in bringing your mind and body back into balance than a good laugh. It lightens your worries, helps you to get on with others and also heightens your awareness. I know this to be true because my family have the wonderful ability to laugh at almost anything. Laughter has seen us through some difficult times and I am pleased to say my grandchildren have developed a terrific sense of humour.

I know I could not live without laughter and it is something I do every day of my life without even thinking about it. Try to shed the more serious side of your nature even if it is only for a few minutes a day. Spend time with friends or loved ones that have that knack of making you laugh.

I remember a good friend of mine had had a serious operation on her back and was in hospital for a couple of months in a plaster cast. I went to visit her on many occasions to help keep her spirits up and was once actually asked to leave – nicely I might add – because I quite literally 'made her laugh too much'! Needless to say, it made her feel good, but the movement the laughter caused was not conducive to the healing of her back. You can't always win, you see.

Did you also know that laughter can help to protect the heart as it improves the function of blood vessels and thus eases the flow of blood? The benefits of laughter seem to stay with you long after the physical act of laughing has subsided. It helps to keep you on top of life and gives you a more positive outlook when faced with what seem to be insurmountable problems.

Laughter can be the missing link in making a relationship work. If you can laugh with each other, even when you feel angry, it will trigger positive feelings and help forge a stronger bond. Laughing with others is far more powerful than laughing on your own and it's a great way of keeping relationships alive and kicking. How many times have you laughed today?

Herbs and Their Medicinal Benefits

In my day herbs were used frequently to treat minor disorders, but it wasn't until recently that I learned their medicinal value. I have always drunk mint tea to alleviate stomach ache, taken echinacea to help build my immune system and rubbed aloe vera gel on mild burns. Since the use of herbs as a treatment for various illnesses has been around for a very long time, I thought I would list a few of their benefits which can often save you a visit to the health centre. If I can find a herb or plant that will benefit my condition, I will always turn to this method before rushing off to the chemist or doctor for a proprietary brand. Many of these remedies can be grown at home and I am never without a couple of aloe vera plants on my kitchen windowsill ready for the next emergency.

Before testing any of the remedies listed in this section, I suggest you first consult your doctor, especially if you are pregnant or suffering from any serious condition for which you are receiving medical attention, as I would not like to be responsible for any adverse reaction. It is always better to be safe than sorry, an expression we were brought up on, and in this case that saying rings particularly true.

If you are gathering your own herbs, make sure you can correctly identify them and never ever pick any from the roadside as these may be contaminated with toxic substances. The safest way is to grow your own herbs not only for cooking but for the medicine cabinet as well, then you know exactly what you are picking and in what conditions it has been grown. I have a separate herb garden that is clearly labelled and I keep a notebook of all their uses so that I have a quick reference if the need arises. Here are a few of the herbs that I have used over the past few years and which I have found extremely beneficial:

HERB	POSSIBLE MEDICINAL USES
Aloe vera	Healing and soothing, particularly for minor burns
Angelica	Aids digestion and helps dispel uncomfortable stomach cramps and flatulence
Arnica	Reduces pain, swelling and bruising
Calendula (marigold)	Helps balance oestrogen levels and promotes healing
Celery	Has anti-inflammatory properties and acts as a diuretic
Chamomile	Soothing sedative
Chicory	Acts as a laxative, a digestive aid and a diuretic
Chilli/cayenne	Acts as an expectorant, decongestant, analgesic, anti-inflammatory, anticoagulant and lowers cholesterol
Dandelion	Excellent diuretic – reduces water retention

HERB	POSSIBLE MEDICINAL USES
Echinacea	By fighting off colds and flu, helps boost the body's immune system and therefore its ability to heal
Fennel	Antispasmodic and helps increase milk flow in nursing mothers
Feverfew	Reduces inflammation, helps to improve circulation and is also beneficial in the treatment of migraines
Garlic	Helps fight off infection and is beneficial in cardiovascular treatments
Ginger	Eases pain from flatulence and diarrhoea, aids digestion and helps quell motion sickness
Lavender	Great at lifting spirits, helps in relaxation and settles the stomach during stress
Lemon Balm	Aids digestion, helps stop stomach cramps and is antiviral
Liquorice root	Acts as an expectorant and also has anti-viral and anti-inflammatory properties
Mint	Aids digestion, reduces flatulence and helps alleviate nausea
Nasturtium	Good source of vitamin C, builds up a resistance to infection

HERB	POSSIBLE MEDICINAL USES
Plantain	Helps to reduce catarrh and also stops bleeding in minor cuts
Raspberry (leaf)	Great for reducing labour and menstrual pains
Rosemary	Improves blood supply to the head
Sage	Helps reduce inflammation in mucous membranes and aids digestion
St John's Wort	Helps with mild depression
Thyme	A good expectorant and also has antibacterial and antifungal properties
Turmeric	Anti-inflammatory and a powerful antioxidant
Witch hazel	Anti-inflammatory and soothes sunburn

Beating the Blues

I imagine that at some stage in your life you have felt down in the dumps, struggling to enjoy life as much as you should. It might be a hormonal problem associated with PMS, post-natal depression or the menopause, or perhaps the result of a trauma that you are finding hard to come to terms with. In severe cases, of course, you will need to consult a doctor, but in mild cases of what we used to call 'the blues' there are things you can do to tackle the negative feelings.

If I had trouble coping when I was a child, say if a big exam was looming or I had been asked to sing a solo for the school, I used to feel a little down in the dumps. Mother would usually say, 'You're making a mountain out of molehill,' which, of course, did nothing to soothe my troubled mind. I like to think I am a little more understanding and, with my knowledge of plants and herbs to hand, try to handle the situation a little more practically. Of course, at my age worries seem a distant memory as I have learned to handle nearly all that life throws at me. After all, life is far too short to worry!

One thing I used to do for my daughter the night before an exam was to give her a nice massage using lavender oil or sage, both of which have a wonderful calming effect. A warm bath and a nice steaming cup of chamomile tea just before bed had a soothing effect, and she said she always slept like a log after one of my 'administrations'. I like to think I followed in the footsteps of the author Beatrix Potter, who frequently mentioned herbs and other plants throughout her books. In *The Tale of Peter Rabbit,* Peter's mother put him to bed with a soothing cup of chamomile tea after his rather disastrous adventure in Mr McGregor's garden.

TRY TO HELP YOURSELF

During times of stress there are several things you can do to try to make yourself feel better without having to resort to a course of antidepressants. Firstly, caffeine tends to have an unsettling effect on the nervous system, so try to reduce your intake to a minimum. Eat plenty of wholefoods, fish that are rich in Omega-3 such as salmon, mackerel, herring, trout, sardines and tuna, and make sure you are including enough protein in your diet. Drink plenty of water to keep your system flushed through and remember sunlight can have a very uplifting effect. Often, minor depression can be associated with a lack of natural daylight, particularly during the winter months. This is referred to as SAD or seasonal affective disorder.

If possible, get as much fresh air and natural light as you can and take a nice invigorating walk to lift your spirits. There is nothing like a spurt of adrenaline to make you feel better. Sitting down and feeling sorry for yourself and eating junk food – as tempting as it may be – is only going to make you feel worse, so 'get up and go' is the key to feeling better. Being in the company of a good friend can help, so why not phone one and ask them to go for a walk with you? Choose the friend who makes you laugh the most and I guarantee by the end of the day you will be wondering what you were worrying about.

Alternatively, try a bout of yoga as this is a well-known Indian antidote to depression.

Mother Nature's First Aid Kit

My grandma seemed to have a solution for most minor accidents that happened to us. She had many dried herbs hanging up in her pantry and numerous bottles with fancy labels on the top shelf. Whether I had tummy ache, an insect sting, a headache or a grazed knee, she would fetch her wooden stool and precariously balance on her toes to reach one of her potent remedies.

Following in her footsteps, I am a firm believer in natural remedies and this has rubbed off on to my children, who have continued in the age-old practice of using herbs whenever possible. Boys will be boys, and my grandsons are constantly grazing their knees and elbows, or bruising themselves as they play at soldiers in the garden. I keep a variety of lotions and potions in the door of my fridge ready for any eventuality.

When they told their friends about my potions, they shocked half the class who instantly imagined that I was a witch. My youngest giggled and told me he had enlarged on the story by telling them I had an enormous wart on the end of my nose and that there was always a large cauldron bubbling on top of the Aga. I wonder where they got their sense of humour from!

ACHES AND PAINS
* Make a warm compress out of lavender, marjoram and thyme and place over the affected area for 15 minutes.
* Bruised, sore muscles and sprains will benefit from being

rubbed with arnica as it has anti-inflammatory properties.
* Soak in a warm bath containing some Epsom salts to help ease away muscular aches and pains.
* Make an infusion of comfrey leaves and apply as a cold compress to sprains and strains.
* Aloe vera is rich in anti-inflammatory substances so use it to help reduce pain and swelling.
* Having a bath which contains a few drops of lavender oil can soak away the aches and pains associated with stress.

BITES AND STINGS

* First check to see if the sting has been left behind in the skin. If so, it should be carefully removed either by using tweezers or flicking it out with the blade of a knife.
* For wasp stings, rub the affected area with either lemon juice or vinegar.
* For bee stings, dilute some bicarbonate of soda in water and rub over the area.
* Fresh onion rubbed on the skin can give quick relief from insect stings.
* For mosquito bites, add tea tree oil or aloe vera gel directly on to the bite.
* For nettle stings, rub the affected area with a dock leaf or lavender oil.

BLISTERS

* Use lavender or tea tree oil diluted in a neutral vegetable oil such as olive, almond or sesame – one part lavender or tea tree to five parts vegetable oil. Apply to the blister and allow to soak in.

✽ Make a salve containing comfrey and spread it on the blister.
✽ If you have some chamomile tea bags, simply moisten one
   and hold it on the blister.
✽ Apply an infusion of St John's Wort, using a clean piece of
   cotton wool several times a day.

BRUISES

✽ Use an ice cold compress made up with some lavender oil to
   avoid swelling and widespread bruising.
✽ Arnica is a well-known remedy for bruises. Apply as a cream
   as long as the skin is not broken.
✽ Witch hazel is another useful herb for bruising. Make up
   some ice cubes containing crushed witch hazel and keep them
   handy to place on top of a bruised area.

BURNS

✽ Aloe vera is a cool and soothing gel that has been used for
   thousands of years to treat minor burns.
✽ Added to a bath, the juice of aloe vera can help relieve the
   discomfort of sunburn.
✽ Lavender oil, with its strong antiseptic properties, can help
   heal burns. If applied quickly, it can help prevent scarring.
✽ Arnica can help take the sting out of minor burns.

COMMON COLD

✽ Citrus fruits – orange, lemon and grapefruit – all have
   healing properties. Orange can bring down a temperature,
   grapefruit can calm a fever and lemon helps to cleanse and
   purify the system.

* Honey can help soothe a sore throat and banish the irritation of a tickly cough. Make a soothing drink of honey and lemon and serve it warm. This can also help to reduce a headache associated with a cold.
* Garlic has antibacterial properties that help the immune system fight off infection. It is a very effective remedy for chest infections, so include garlic in your diet to help prevent colds.
* Rosemary can ease headaches if drunk as a tea, or sore throats if used as a gargle.
* Sage tea is also good for treating head colds and restoring the appetite.
* Eucalyptus can help clear catarrh from the head and sinuses. A few drops on a tissue or handkerchief inhaled at regular intervals can help relieve the discomfort of nasal congestion.

CUTS AND GRAZES
* Tea tree oil has both antiseptic and antifungal properties which make it ideal for treating minor cuts and grazes.
* Extra virgin olive oil that has been slighlty warmed can be applied directly to damaged skin. The astringent and antiseptic qualities in olives help to clean and protect the wound from infection.
* Soak 4 teaspoons of red clover flowers in a pint of hot water for 10 minutes. Allow it to cool and then soak some cottonwool in the liquid and apply directly to the wound.
* Boil a handful of lavender flowers in a pint of water, allow the mixture to cool and then strain and dab on to the skin using clean cottonwool.

HANGOVER

I imagine that most people have suffered from a hangover at
least once in their life. If you have never had one, then consider
yourself lucky. I learned my lesson after the first time, but
for those of you who constantly make the same mistake then
remember, you are never too old to learn. The main symptoms
are dehydration, a dry mouth, tiredness, headache and nausea,
all of which are caused because you have destroyed the natural
balance of your body. Try one of these cures, which will
hopefully lessen the severity of your suffering.

* Bananas are high in potassium, so eating one for breakfast can
  help balance the body salts.
* Dandelion is a great remedy for hangovers as it is one of the
  few diuretics that also adds potassium back into the body. It is a
  brilliant detoxifier as it helps to eliminate the bad toxins caused
  by drinking. Either eat some in a salad or make a dandelion tea,
  which you can sweeten to make it more palatable.
* Chamomile tea is a general soother and helps your body to
  relax. It works wonders on the hangover headache and helps
  to settle the stomach, especially when sweetened with honey.
* Drink a lukewarm cup of fennel tea to help overcome nausea.
* Lemon and lime are two of nature's natural refreshers, so a
  glass of cool water mixed with the juice of either of these will
  act as a pick-me-up.
* Make an infusion using mint or chew on a fresh leaf to
  calm the stomach, freshen your rather stale breath and
  ease a headache.
* Rosemary is a natural stimulant. Either use it in the bath or
  chop some over a salad to relieve feelings of tiredness.

If none of the above has any effect on your hangover, then I suggest you tell everyone to leave you alone and go back to bed to wallow in your self-induced suffering.

HAYFEVER
* Take echinacea every day to boost the immune system in time for the hayfever season.
* Add garlic to your diet one or two months before the hayfever season begins.
* Chamomile can help soothe red and itchy eyes. Make a weak cup of chamomile tea, allow to cool and then soak a couple of cottonwool pads in the solution. Gently place over the eyes and leave until the soreness has subsided.
* Nettles are full of chlorophyl and formic acid, both of which help to strengthen the immune system against hayfever. They can either be made into a tea or eaten as a spring vegetable.
* A herbal infusion of elderflowers is both an excellent preventative measure and treatment for hayfever.

HEADACHE
* If you are suffering from a tension headache, the first thing you need to do is to try and relax. Dip a flannel in some ice-cold water and place it over the area of pain. Lie down, close your eyes and take yourself to a 'happy place'.
* If you are experiencing nausea with your headache, try drinking a glass of pure peach juice to settle your stomach.
* Dab a few drops of peppermint oil on your forehead to try and ease a tension headache. But be warned: do not use on children or on anyone with sensitive skin as it can have a burning effect.

❊ Make a scented bag out of dried marjoram, rosemary and mint. Whenever you feel a headache coming on, hold the little sachet up to your nose and inhale deeply until you feel the pain subsiding.

❊ Drink an infusion of 1 teaspoon of crushed rosemary leaves and 1 teaspoon crushed sage leaves in a cup of boiling water. Cover the cup and allow to steep until the tea reaches room temperature. Strain and drink in half cup doses two to three times a day.

❊ Make a compress by putting 5 drops of lavender essential oil in cold water. Soak a soft cloth and put it on your forehead.

Remember, if you frequently suffer from severe headaches make sure you take a trip to the doctor as it might be the symptom of a more serious problem.

NOSEBLEED

❊ Put a drop or two of lemon juice in the nostril that is bleeding.

❊ Dissolve a pinch of salt in half a glass of water and spray it inside the nostril.

❊ Soak a cotton bud in apple cider vinegar and apply it to the bleeding nostril. This will help the blood to congeal.

❊ Apply an icepack to the bridge of the nose. This should quickly stem the bleeding.

❊ A wet towel placed on the head has also been found to be beneficial in curing a nosebleed.

❊ Because a dry atmosphere can cause a nosebleed, try to make sure the room the patient is in is moist. You can do this by boiling a kettle or sitting them in the bathroom with a bath full of hot water.

RASHES AND IRRITATIONS

Skin allergies can be caused by any number of things – a change in temperature, allergies to certain foods or drugs, pollen, household dust or perfumed soap products like washing powders. If you have recently started using something different or eating something that you wouldn't normally have, then try to isolate what you think the problem might be. Avoid using anything scented on your skin or hair and avoid using make-up until the problem has gone away. Avoid wearing any jewellery that contains nickel as this can often irritate the skin. Try some of the following to help relieve the irritation.

* Witch hazel acts as an astringent that will relieve the itching. For best results try and obtain fresh witch hazel bark. Simmer 1 oz of bark in 1 pint of water and leave for ten minutes. Strain and allow to cool. Apply with clean cottonwool and leave it on the skin for 30 minutes.
* Aloe vera gel works well in soothing skin irritations. Slice off a portion of the leaf and apply the gel directly to the affected area.
* Calendula oil is often used to reduce the inflammation of nappy rash. You can use the actual herb by putting 2 teaspoons of calendula in a cup of boiling water. Leave it to simmer for about ten minutes and apply to the affected area once the mixture has cooled to body temperature.
* Pour some boiling water over a bowl of rolled oats. Cover the bowl and leave to soak for ten minutes. Strain the water and pour into an ice cube tray. Freeze and use the ice cubes to relieve the itching by gently rubbing them over the affected area.

STOMACH UPSETS AND INDIGESTION

✳ Place 1 teaspoon of caraway seeds in a cup and add boiling water. Allow it to stand for ten minutes, strain well and drink up to three cups a day on an empty stomach. Alternatively, you can simply chew on a few seeds after dinner to try and avoid indigestion.

✳ Cinnamon is great at stimulating the digestive system. You can make a pleasant tea by stirring ½ teaspoon of ground cinnamon into 1 cup of hot water. Allow to stand for five minutes before drinking.

✳ Fennel is a wonderful herb for calming gas and stomach cramps. Make a tea using 1 teaspoon of fennel seeds to a cup of boiling water. Allow to stand for ten minutes and then strain before drinking on an empty stomach.

✳ Ginger has been used for centuries to help stomach ailments of all types, particularly nausea. Add ½ teaspoon of ground ginger to a cup of boiling water and allow to stand for three minutes before drinking.

✳ Many proprietary medicines for upset stomach are flavoured with mint and this is because mint helps food move through the intestines properly, which aids digestion. Make a mint tea by putting a sprig of mint in a cup and adding boiling water. Leave to infuse for ten minutes, strain and drink, preferably on an empty stomach.

✳ Stomach cramps can be caused by a lack of fibre in the diet, so make sure you get plenty of fibre by regularly eating an apple and a banana, and include other fibre-rich foods in your diet, such as oats, beans and lentils.

Growing Old Gracefully

I wouldn't be doing my job if I didn't add a section on how to ease yourself gently into the ageing process. As you get older your metabolism starts to slow down, which causes your energy levels to drop. In the case of women, they have to cope with the symptoms of the menopause or 'change of life', as some people like to call it: the time that signals the end of your reproductive years. Some women sail through this without any bother and relish the thought of not having to cope with monthly periods. Other women are not so lucky and suffer uncomfortable symptoms such as hot flushes, anxiety, insomnia and depression. Although many women choose to undergo hormone replacement therapy (HRT), there are other things we can do to cut down on the amount of suffering. Once again, I cannot stress enough that a good diet and regular exercise can help keep you feeling young.

Keeping your joints moving is vital to try and delay the onset of rheumatism, arthritis, gout and brittle bones, which in themselves can be incapacitating but can also lead to depression as people suffer constant pain and lack of mobility. There are many natural ways to help these conditions and also to improve memory loss and circulation.

I realized that my body was slowing down when I could no longer leap over stiles when out walking the dogs. Today, I take it slowly and ease my old bones over any stile, although I consider myself lucky that I have managed to remain active enough to still be able to play most of the games with my family. Because I am a big child at heart, my grandchildren like me to be part of their games when they come to stay. Being fit enough to play with them is only possible because I manage to sustain a reasonable diet along with a sensible fitness regime.

THE INCREDIBLE POWERS OF CELERY

Celery is one of the most nutritious foods we can eat, whether we eat it raw or drink it as a juice. It levels out the body's pH balance, improves circulation, detoxifies the blood and prevents uric acid from damaging the joints, which is the main cause of gout, arthritis and rheumatism. This vegetable is rich in vitamins, potassium, folic acid, calcium, magnesium, iron, phosphorus, sodium and essential amino acids. It also contains essential oils which help to regulate the nervous system. Celery contains natural organic sodium (or salt) which is safe for consumption and is, in fact, essential for the body. Natural sodium, unlike iodized sodium (table salt), is safe even for those with high blood pressure. It also contains compounds that help fight off cancer and lower cholesterol. It can aid digestion, rehydrate and also act as a diuretic. Because it is an anti-inflammatory it can bring relief to people with rheumatoid arthritis, gout and osteoarthritis if taken regularly. The juice is the most efficient and nutritious way of taking celery, and you can be comfortable in the fact that you can drink as much as you like without fear of overloading your system. Celery is indeed the most useful vegetable in helping to fight problems associated with getting older.

Apart from celery, there are other herbs which can benefit those approaching their twilight years:

Rosemary contains four anti-inflammatory substances which help with problems associated with the joints. It also improves circulation to the brain, which helps boost that fading memory and increase alertness.

Purple sage, red clover and *liquorice* all contain a substance similar to oestrogen that can help to strengthen bones and possibly increase bone density.

Hot flushes can be eased by taking vitamin E, and foods that are rich in this include:

sunflower oil	margarine	pine nuts
hazelnuts	brazil nuts	popcorn
almonds	marzipan	avocado
rapeseed oil	sweet potato	peanuts
cod liver oil	Walnuts	flapjacks
mayonnaise	egg yolks	muesli

SOMETHING FOR THE MEN

I must include something here for the men. I wouldn't like anyone to think that they weren't worth considering when it comes to the ageing process. One thing that older men need to be concerned about is prostate problems. Normally the size of a walnut, the prostate can become enlarged, which can cause uncomfortable urinary problems.

❋ One of the best natural remedies for prostate problems is to eat pumpkin seeds as they are a rich source of unsaturated fatty acid. This is vital to the health of the prostate, so eat 50 g (3 oz) daily either as a snack or cooked in food.

* Zinc is very beneficial in keeping the prostate in good order so eat plenty of foods that are rich in this mineral. They include:

oysters	cheese
beef (organic)	almonds, cashews, pecans
crab	milk
pork (organic)	kidney beans
chicken (organic)	peas
lobster	oatmeal
yogurt	flounder or sole
chickpeas	ginger root

* Drink plenty of vegetable juice, such as spinach and carrot, and fruit juices, such as apple, mango, pear and orange.
* Eat plenty of foods that contain vitamin E. See page 57 for a list of these.
* Reduce your intake of caffeine and try to limit the amount of alcohol you drink.
* Drink plenty of water to keep your body hydrated, which will also help flush out any impurities and toxins.
* Hydrotherapy treatment also helps – use alternating hot and cold water for the lower abdomen, either using a shower or by sitting in the bath.

'DODDER NOT' CAKE

Yes, there is actually a recipe for a cake that can help you fight the signs of ageing. This cake, which my own grandma named 'Dodder Not' because she refused to become 'doddery', is rich in ingredients that have high levels of phyto-oestrogens – put simply, nature's version of our own hormone oestrogen.

100 g (4 oz) soya flour	2 pieces finely chopped stem
100 g (4 oz) wholemeal flour	ginger
100 g (4 oz) rolled oats	225 g (8 oz) raisins, dates or
100 g (4 oz) linseeds	cranberries
50 g (2 oz) pumpkin seeds	½ tsp nutmeg
50 g (2 oz) flaked almonds	½ tsp cinnamon
50 g (2 oz) sesame seeds	½ tsp ground ginger
50 g (2 oz) sunflower seeds	425 ml (15 fl oz) soya milk

✻ *Put all the dry ingredients into a large bowl. Add the soya milk and mix well. Leave to soak for about one hour.*

✻ *Preheat the oven to 190°C/375°F/Gas mark 5.*

✻ *Line a small loaf tin with baking parchment.*

✻ *Spoon the mixture into the prepared tin. The mixture should be a soft, dropping consistency, so if it is too thick just add a little more soya milk.*

✻ *Bake for 1 to 1½ hours and then test with a skewer to check if it has cooked through.*

✻ *Turn the cake out on to a rack and allow to cool.*

Eat a slice a day to keep old age at bay.

MANAGING
THE HOME

Cleaning the Natural Way

As a young child I was always encouraged – not forced, mind you – to help with chores around the house. Mother and Father were busy working, Mother as a primary school teacher and Father fighting for his country. Grandma basically ran the house while my grandpa looked after the 'outside jobs', as he called them. Everything always looked spick and span and there was always a lovely dinner waiting on the table when we came home from school.

Grandma's cleaning tools were what we would consider today eco-friendly and far cheaper than the vast array of cleaning products that we face on our supermarket shelves – one for cleaning the bath, one for cleaning the toilet, one for cleaning windows, one for cleaning the cooker and so on and so forth. In my day it was far less complicated. We used items that we had in our pantry, such as:

* Vinegar
* Lemon
* Bicarbonate of soda
* Cream of tartar
* Washing soda
* Borax
* Salt
* Mild organic soap
* Lavender (or your favourite) essential oil

Follow this strategy and not only do your cupboards remain uncluttered by lots of different cleaning products, but you are causing less pollution, the items you use are less toxic and they have been tried and tested for generations. On top of that you are saving a lot of money. What other reasons do you need?

Even though these products are natural I would still suggest wearing rubber gloves when doing the cleaning, as they can be quite harsh on delicate skin if used regularly.

There is no need to buy endless disposable cloths for cleaning either, just find an old cotton sheet, cut it up into squares and, if you want to be really posh, quickly sew round the edges to stop them fraying. Cotton can be washed time and time again, so your cloths should last for quite a while.

I want to approach the next few pages as if I was doing my annual spring clean. By that, I mean a thorough refreshing of the whole house. I am going to include some simple recipes and tips to help you and then you can sit down with a nice cup of tea and pat yourself on the back. They say cleanliness is next to godliness, so let's get started.

LET THE FRESH AIR IN

Our first job is to go round and open as many windows as possible to let out the winter stuffiness. Throw out those nasty, synthetic air fresheners because – did you know? – they can trigger allergic reactions such as asthma, skin and respiratory irritation and headaches. A vase of beautiful cut flowers will do exactly the same job, provided, of course, that you do not suffer from hayfever. If that is the case then put a few drops of your favourite essential oil on some cottonwool balls and leave them in inconspicuous places.

Now let's get down to the nitty gritty and do some actual cleaning. I am going to give you a few tips for making your own cleaners and I know you will be amazed at the results you can achieve with very little effort.

ALL-PURPOSE CLEANER
2 tbsps bicarbonate of soda
1 pint warm water
Juice of half a lemon
1 tbsp white vinegar

Mix all the above together in a spray bottle and use anywhere that you want to give a really good clean. The lemon and vinegar are mild acids that really help to cut through the grease.

If you have a spot that needs a little abrasive action, say in the kitchen, then mix up some bicarbonate of soda with sufficient liquid soap to form a paste. Only mix a little at a time as this dries up very quickly.

NO-STREAK WINDOW CLEANER
1 pint warm water
250 ml white vinegar

Mix the two ingredients in a spray bottle and spray on to the glass in your window. Wipe over with a sponge and then crumple up some old newspapers and wipe off the excess. To leave your windows with a really sparkling clean finish, use a bit more elbow grease and continue buffing up the glass with the newspaper.

NON-TOXIC TOILET CLEANER

There is no need to use harsh bleaches in your toilet to get it really clean. Simply flush your toilet so the sides of the pan are wet and then sprinkle some borax around the bowl. Next, spray some white vinegar around the bowl, leave for a couple of hours and then scrub gently to remove stains.

If you have some really stubborn stains, try a paste of lemon juice and borax which you can rub on the stains – leave for 30 minutes before removing.

SINK AND BATH TAPS

If you have a build-up of mineral deposits round your taps, soak some paper towels in neat vinegar and wrap around the base. Leave for at least one hour and then you will find the deposits wipe away with ease.

VENETIAN BLINDS

Venetian blinds harbour dust and dirt and are not the easiest things to clean. I found a good way of getting round this problem by folding a slice of new bread in half and rubbing it over each individual slat. As the bread becomes really dirty, discard it and start with a fresh piece.

CHEMICAL-FREE OVEN CLEANER

My first suggestion would be to make a natural oven cleaner by mixing about 5 tablespoons of bicarbonate of soda, a few drops of liquid soap and approximately 4 tablespoons of white vinegar into a thick paste. Put on some rubber gloves and apply the paste to the inside of the oven. Scrub any stubborn marks with an abrasive sponge and then rinse and wipe clean.

If your oven is particularly greasy, then you can use some lemon and salt. Mix equal parts of lemon juice and salt and cover the stains. Leave for 30 minutes, scrub with an abrasive sponge, rinse and wipe the oven clean.

FRIDGE CLEANER
All you need to clean your fridge is a cloth soaked in a strong solution of bicarbonate of soda and hot water. This will absorb any nasty odours and leave your fridge smelling really fresh without contaminating any of the food.

DEFUR YOUR KETTLE
If you find your kettle has become furred up with a build-up of limescale, the simple solution is to half fill it with equal quantities of water and vinegar and boil. Once the water has boiled, leave it to do its magic for about 15 minutes, then rinse it out thoroughly and boil with clean water. You may need to boil it with clean water a couple of times to make sure you totally get rid of the taste of vinegar. The vinegar won't do you any harm, but it is not very conducive to a nice cup of tea.

KITCHEN WORKTOPS
If you have any stubborn marks on your worktop you needn't reach for one of those cleaners that say 'added bleach'. Simply leave a puddle of lemon juice over the mark and rinse off after a couple of hours.

POTS AND PANS
If some of your pots and pans need a bit of a facelift, then simply fill with water and add some white vinegar. Boil for

several minutes and then rinse thoroughly. If you have some saucepans with copper bottoms, the easiest way to get these looking like new is to rub them with a little tomato ketchup. I know this sounds strange, but trust me – it works.

If you have any plastic containers that have absorbed the smell of food, then leave them overnight in a solution of bicarbonate of soda and water. Rinse thoroughly and they should smell sweet and fresh.

DEODORIZE YOUR CARPET

You can quickly make your carpets smell cleaner by liberally sprinkling them with bicarbonate of soda. Wait for 15 minutes and then simply vacuum up the powder – much cheaper and more effective than buying that well-known brand of expensive carpet freshener.

FURNITURE POLISH

One of the best furnitures polishes I have ever used on any type of wood is a mixture of two parts olive oil to one part lemon juice. You simply apply a thin layer and then buff it up using a soft cloth. It gives you a really natural, fresh finish.

METAL POLISH

The easiest way to clean copper and brass is to polish it with a paste of lemon juice and salt. Rinse clean and buff up to a shine.

Silver can be boiled in water that contains 1 teaspoon of bicarbonate of soda, 1 teaspoon of salt and a small piece of kitchen foil. If you need to get into any awkward places, use an old toothbrush and rub with a paste of bicarbonate of soda and water. Rinse thoroughly and polish with a soft cloth.

REFRESH THAT MATTRESS

The next time you need to change your bed, take off the mattress cover too and sprinkle some bicarbonate of soda mixed with some crushed lavender flowers directly on to the mattress. Go away and do some other chores for a couple of hours and then simply come back and vacuum away the mixture. This will not only leave your mattress smelling fresh but it will do wonders for your hoover as well.

Lavender is known to induce relaxation so why not leave a few flowerheads under your pillow for a relaxing night's sleep. If possible, always allow your sheets to dry on a line in the sun. There is nothing nicer than climbing into a freshly made bed that smells of fresh air.

If your child has had a little accident and wet the bed, the best way to get rid of the smell is to sprinkle some dry borax over the wet spot, allow it to dry and vacuum off.

SMELLY DRAINS

If your drains are giving off a nasty odour, then pour some bicarbonate of soda followed by a cupful of vinegar directly down the plughole. Put the plug in and leave the two components to react with one another for about 30 minutes. Pour a kettle full of boiling water down the drain to wash away any nasty residue.

COBWEBS

Cobwebs seem to pop up overnight and there is nothing we can actually do to prevent them. If you do not have an extension to your hoover that can reach high enough, then I have always found the good old feather duster the best solution. Just twist and the cobweb will wind itself round the feathers.

Washday Tips

I don't know about you, but in my house there seems to be a never-ending stream of washing – where does it all come from? I decided a few years ago I somehow needed to cut down on the money I spent on detergent and fabric conditioner and decided to go back to some old-fashioned methods. Actually, I was quite astonished at how well they worked. Not only did my laundry smell really fresh, but I didn't have to compromise on the final result either. Like many other people, I believed that you had to have a really powerful biological detergent to get clothes thoroughly clean, but this really isn't the case. You don't need boiling hot water either, so you can save some pennies there as well because your washing machine won't have to work so hard to heat the water.

Make sure you don't overload the washing machine because your clothes will not get clean if there is insufficient room in the drum. Also make sure that the load is evenly distributed so that heavy items do not cause undue pressure during the spin cycle as this will cause wear and tear to both your clothes and the machine.

Pre-soak any really dirty or stained items in washing soda before putting them in the machine.

Make sure you keep your washing machine running efficiently by cleaning it once a month. This can easily be done by placing some washing soda directly in the drum and then running it on one of the hot wash cycles.

RECIPE FOR NATURAL WASHING POWDER

Using a regular household cup, measure out the following:

1 cup white vinegar
1 cup of bicarbonate of soda
1 cup of washing soda
¼ cup of liquid soap

Pour the liquid soap into a bowl, stir in the washing soda followed by the bicarbonate of soda. Gradually add the vinegar and stir; the mixture will start to foam at this stage and then turn into a thick paste. Once it has broken down it will dry into a heavy powdered detergent if you keep stirring. If you find any hard lumps, try to break them down while stirring. Store in a sealed container and use as you would a normal washing powder.

NATURAL FABRIC CONDITIONER

All you need for a natural fabric conditioner is some white vinegar. By adding a cup to the final rinse it not only gets rid of any nasty smells and softens the clothes, it also helps eliminate any build-up of soap residue as well.

Here are some more washday tips to make your life easier and help you save some money into the bargain. It really is worth giving them a try – these old tried and tested methods really do work best.

* Clothes dry most economically in the fresh air and sunlight as this has a natural deodorizing and purifying effect. Much cheaper than using a tumble dryer and your clothes will last longer too.

* If you have any permanent-press items, only wash them on a cool wash, otherwise you will find it impossible to remove the creases.

* Wash and dry denim jeans inside out to stop them fading.

* Make sure any zips are done up before washing items, such as trousers, as the teeth on metal zips can quickly wear holes in other items of clothing.

* Any small items like baby's socks should always be washed in a laundry bag so they are not lost in the water outlet hose of the washing machine.

* Always wash bras in a laundry bag so that the hook cannot snag other clothes or get caught in the holes in the drum of the washing machine.

* Reduce static by adding white vinegar to the final rinse.

* If you live in a hard water area, add some borax to soften the water and it will help to make your clothes white as well.

* If you are forced to use the tumble dryer during a spell of inclement weather, then make sure you always use dryer balls. You can easily make your own by rolling up a sheet of tin foil into a ball.

* When washing new towels leave them to soak for ten minutes in a solution of white vinegar and water before putting them on a normal washing cycle. This will help the colours to set.

* If you find that your blacks are fading to greys, you can quickly restore their colour by adding some black coffee or strong black tea to the final rinse water.

❀ Make sure you always sort your laundry into coloureds and whites so that you do not run the risk of colours ruining the lighter fabrics.

❀ Conventional stain removers are too harsh and can damage your clothes, so try using a paste made out of bicarbonate of soda and water and scrub the affected area before washing.

❀ To remove ink stains from a garment, soak just the stained area in a bowl of fresh milk before washing.

NATURAL IRONING TIPS

❀ If you have a sticky build-up on the plate of your iron, turn it to its highest setting and then pour a small amount of salt on to a sheet of greaseproof paper. Run the hot iron back and forth over the paper until all the residue has gone.

❀ If your clothes are too dry and full of creases, try laying a damp towel on the ironing board first and then place the clothes on top of the towel. The steam coming from the hot iron and from the hot wet towel below will quickly get rid of those stubborn creases.

❀ Make sure you iron any delicate fabrics inside out to prevent getting those nasty shiny marks.

❀ The easiest way to tackle a shirt is to iron the collar first, then the sleeves and finally the body.

❀ If you need to let down a hem on an item of clothing, soak a clean cloth in a mixture of equal parts water and white vinegar. Lay the cloth over the old hem, fold and iron over the cloth.

❀ If you need to starch something like a linen tablecloth or napkins, make your own mixture by adding 1 tablespoon of cornflour to 1 pint of cold water into a spray bottle. Spray the fabric all over before ironing.

Gran'll Fix It

I don't think it is always necessary to call on a 'handy man' to get those little jobs done around the house. All you need is a little know-how and the right tool for the job. If you keep a neat and tidy tool box with some basic equipment, then you should have everything handy to do some simple home repairs. Make sure they are somewhere you can reach them without having to empty half the contents of a cupboard or shed and then the task will not seem quite so daunting. These are the items I have found most useful over the years, so I suggest you make a start with these. You can always build up your collection once your confidence grows. Another little word of advice is to make sure you keep your tools in good condition. Keep joints regularly oiled and then you won't be frustrated by stiff, rusty tools if you haven't used them for a long time. Remember, a bad workman always blames his tools, so make sure your tools are in tip-top condition; otherwise you only have yourself to blame if something goes wrong.

BASIC TOOL KIT
You can either buy an expensive measuring tape or you can do as I do and use an old cloth

one. This is small enough to put in your pocket if you have to go shopping and you need to make sure that it will fit.

* You will need two types of screwdrivers, one with a flat head and one cross head. You can buy convenient kits with interchangeable heads which means you will always have the right size for the job at hand. I always keep a tiny set of screwdrivers in my kitchen drawer for tightening my glasses, which, for some strange reason, keep coming loose. Might be because I keep forgetting where I put them and often end up sitting on them!

* Buy yourself a pair of pliers. The slip-joint plier is the one I would choose if you are only going to buy one as it is versatile and can handle a variety of jobs.
* I would suggest that you buy a pair of wire-cutters too, as these are invaluable when it comes to changing a plug, snipping wire for craft projects or other household and gardening jobs.
* I know I cannot work without a spirit level because my eyes always seem to deceive me and tell me that something is level when it is not. A good sturdy one will last you a lifetime and will make sure your shelves, pictures, towel rails and anything else you want, are perfectly straight.
* One hammer should do the job, and I would suggest a medium-sized one that is not too heavy to handle comfortably.
* Make sure that you always have a good selection of nails and screws. You can buy a custom assortment already divided

into sizes in a convenient plastic box at your local DIY store. Also make sure you have some rawl plugs, as you will need to place these in the wall before inserting a screw. You can buy a box of assorted sizes to suit most jobs.

* I like to keep a roll of masking tape in my toolbox as this comes in really handy if you are doing any painting or varnishing. It is especially useful if you are painting windows and don't want to get an excess of paint on the glass. It is easier to peel off some tape than embark on the tedious job of scraping paint off a window.

* You will also need a drill and assorted drill bits. If you can stretch to it, I would suggest that you buy an electric drill as it takes the hard work out of making holes.

* Also keep a sharpened pencil in your toolbox as you will need to mark drill holes etc.

If you are intending to do some decorating – and, believe me, this really isn't the daunting task you think it is if you treat it in a methodical way – buy yourself some good-quality brushes so that they don't leave those horrible stray hairs in your newly painted door, a roller and roller tray for doing larger areas and, crucially, a large dust sheet for covering up furniture and carpets.

If you are painting skirting boards, you can use your masking tape on the edge of the carpet to protect it.

Also remember to keep your cats and dogs out of the room you have just painted, otherwise you could end up with a stripey animal and clumps of animal hair stuck to the fixtures and fittings!

THE EASY WAY TO HANG WALLPAPER
Wallpaper is not nearly as difficult to hang as most people believe. I know the first time I tried, I was surprised just how easily I managed on my own despite the fact that I am only five foot nothing.

The secret to successful wallpaper hanging is not to take any shortcuts, be methodical and follow a set pattern to make sure you don't make any mistakes.

Make sure you use a sturdy pair of step ladders and that they are in the right position before climbing up with your first roll of paper. For safety's sake, get someone to hold the ladder and don't try to overreach yourself.

* Firstly, make sure your walls are in good condition. Remove any old wallpaper thoroughly, fill any cracks and sand down any uneven areas.
* You will find it much easier to hang wallpaper if you prime the walls first. Oil-based primers are definitely the best and you need to leave the surface to dry for 24 hours before you start hanging the paper.
* Make sure you buy enough paper to finish the job as there is nothing more frustrating than running out halfway along a wall.
* This next step is very important to ensure that your first sheet of paper is straight. Measure the width of your wallpaper and hang a plumb line from the ceiling as a guideline. Then get someone to mark a vertical line with a pencil down the wall.
* Now you need to measure and cut your first strip of wallpaper. Measure the height of the wall and add a further three inches.

* If you are using one of the modern prepasted wallpapers, you will need to dip the paper into a tray of water and then roll the wallpaper with the pattern facing inwards. Leave the paper in the water for 30 seconds, then remove it and set it on a flat surface such as a pasting table. Fold the wallpaper so that the pasted sides are sticking together, and be careful not to crease it. Leave the paper for about five minutes before hanging on the wall.

* Unfold the wallpaper and place it on the wall to the left-hand side of the pencil line. The wallpaper should slightly overlap at the ceiling and at the skirting board. Using a large wallpaper brush or sponge, carefully smooth the wallpaper over the wall from the top to the bottom. Wipe off any excess paste with a clean cloth.

* Using a straight edge such as a wall scraper, gently push the excess into the angle where the ceiling meets the wall and repeat at the top of the skirting board. Gently peel the paper away from the wall and, using a large pair of wallpaper scissors, cut along the marked crease. Next, using your brush, stick the wallpaper back at the top and bottom and you have completed your first strip.

* Continue round the room making sure that the edges do not overlap and that the pattern lines up where the two strips come together.

* To paper over light switches, lay the strip of paper as normal, then use a sharp blade to cut a cross over the top of the switch. Using the brush push the paper round the edges and then trim using a sharp blade or stanley knife.

Stand back and admire your handywork. See – easy, wasn't it?

HOW TO UNBLOCK A DRAIN

A common household problem is blocked sinks, particularly in the kitchen where the risk of greasy food can build up in the soakaway. By far the easiest and most effective way of dealing with this problem is to use a plunger.

To make sure that the plunger works efficiently, the head needs to totally cover the plug hole. Now gently push the plunger up and down so that a vaccuum is created. This suction should pull any dislodged material that is blocking your sink out of the pipe. If your sink is fitted with an overflow outlet, you will need to block this with a wet sponge or cloth before proceeding with the plunger.

HOW TO CHANGE A PLUG OR FUSE

Plugs sometimes need attention because they have become damaged or because a fuse needs changing. Firstly, it is a good idea to accustom yourself to the colours of wire used inside a plug. These are not the same in all countries, so check the colour codes where you are before you start. Here is a rough guide:

Neutral (N): blue or black (white for USA)
Live (L): brown on red (black, red or blue for USA)
Earth (E): Green and Yellow or plain green

Unscrew and remove the plug cover. If the wires have worked themselves loose from the terminals, undo the screw on the top of the terminal, push the wire inside and tighten the screw down again to hold it tight. There should also be a cable grip where the cable enters the plug, which should be screwed down to hold the cable tight. The fuse can be hooked out with a small screwdriver and replaced with one of the same rating, e.g. 5 amp or 13 amp. Some modern appliances come with a moulded plug which cannot be opened. You will find the fuse cartridge situated in the middle of the pins, and it can be levered out with a small screwdriver. Always screw the plug cover securely back in place before plugging into the main. And if you have any doubts about what you're doing, ask an electrician.

RESTORING FURNITURE

If a favourite piece of furniture is starting to look shabby, you can save yourself quite a lot of money by tackling the simpler jobs yourself. For example, if you want to make a faded surface on top of a wooden table or cabinet come to life, simply mix one part linseed oil with four parts of white spirit. Wipe on and leave for a few minutes, then take off the old wax with another cloth. Once the surface is dry and clean, give it a couple of coats of polish and buff up to a shine.

If you have drawers that keep sticking, you can make them run smoothly again by rubbing a candle along the bottom of the drawer sides.

If you have loose drawer fronts, then scrape off the old glue with a sharp knife and spread new PVA wood glue on the surfaces. Hold the two pieces together using a clamp until the glue has set.

Leather sofas and chairs all too often become dull and scratched from daily use. You do not need to buy expensive leather cleaner: vinegar and olive oil will do the trick. Fill an old jam jar with one third vinegar and top up with olive oil and give it a good shake. You will find a little of this mixture goes a long way so there is no need to soak your sponge. Just a few drops rubbed over the surface of the leather should revive it by removing the surface grime. Then all you have to do is buff it up again with a clean cloth. The vinegar lifts the dirt and the olive oil nourishes the leather.

USEFUL TIPS

I want to end the DIY section with a few useful tips that I have picked up over the years. I hope you will find them beneficial too.

* If you are drilling into brick or plaster walls indoors, use the nozzle on your vacuum cleaner to suck up the dust as you are drilling and then you won't have a nasty mess to clean up. Alternatively, you can hold a dustpan underneath or an open envelope to catch the dust.

* To make screws easier to remove at a later date, rub some soap over the thread before screwing them in.

* If you are screwing into wood, first dip screws in some grease (petroleum jelly will do) to make life easier. Alternatively, you can use a small piece of wax furniture polish in the hole before inserting the screw.

* Do you find you keep hitting your finger or thumb when you try hammering in small tacks or nails? You can get round this by using the teeth of a comb to steady the nail while you hammer it in.

* If you regularly use matches, don't throw them away, cut off the burnt end and use them as rawlplugs or tile spacers.

* If you are using wood filler you can make a better colour match by mixing in a little instant coffee powder with the filler. It won't be nearly so obvious that you have just carried out a repair.

* If you haven't quite finished painting and want to continue the next day, there is no need to wash out the paint tray each time. By placing the whole tray inside a plastic bag and sealing the end with an elastic band, the tray will still be OK to use the next day as the paint will not have dried.
* When using sealant around a bath or sink, fill the bath with water first to stop the bath breaking away from the sealant with the extra weight.
* If you need to drill through a wall to pass an electric cable from one room to another, make sure you drill in the direction the cable is going to run as this will make it feed through much more smoothly.
* If you are fed up with your old kitchen cabinets, there is no need to go to the expense of replacing the whole unit, just replace the doors as the carcasses are nearly always the same. Alternatively, just replace the handles or add stencils to make them look more interesting.
* If you need to measure a round object, take a piece of string and wrap it around the object, marking where both ends meet. Lay the piece of string out flat on a table and then measure it with a tape measure or rule.
* If you need to drill into tiles, stick a piece of masking tape on to the tile first to prevent the drill bit from slipping.
* If you need to drill a hole to a specific depth, the safest thing to do is to place a piece of masking tape around the drill bit at the required depth. As soon as the drill reaches the tape, you know you have reached the desired depth.
* If you suddenly find your toilet will not flush and there is a queue outside the door, don't panic. Simply fill a bucket with water and swill the contents down the toilet bowl.

Safety First

I am sure you probably think your home is a safe place, but it certainly makes you think twice when grandchildren come along or you have an elderly relative come to stay. Here are some useful tips to make your house a safer place – after all there's no use in shutting the stable door after the horse has bolted. In other words, make sure you take the necessary precautions to prevent a nasty accident.

These tips are in no specific order, but just work methodically around the house and use the tick boxes here to make sure that you have taken all the necessary steps to make your house as safe as possible.

❏ Cover any electrical sockets with childproof covers.

❏ Make sure that hallways, stairs and all exits are clearly lit and free of any obstructions.

❏ Only use mats that have a non-skid backing and make sure there are no upturned or frayed corners which could cause a nasty fall.

❏ Use nonskid mats on the base of the bathtub or shower.

❏ Put grab bars on the side of the bath to help elderly persons lever themselves out to save the embarrassment of having to ask for help.

❏ Tell the rest of the family not to use bath oils when bathing as this will make the surface even more slippery.

❏ Turn down the thermostat by a few degrees on your water heater to prevent scalding.

❏ Make sure you have child safety locks or bars on upstairs windows.

❏ Make sure you install smoke alarms and do regular checks to check the batteries do not need replacing.

❏ Make sure you have a firm handrail running up the side of the stairs and that the carpet is not loose on any of the treads. Also make sure the stairs are well lit.

❏ Make sure any medications are locked away out of reach of any children.

❏ Shorten any cords on window blinds to prevent strangulation hazards.

❏ If you have clear glass in your patio doors, make sure you stick some decorations on them so that there is no risk of your child running into them by mistake.

❏ Where necessary, make use of safety gates at the top and bottom of your stairs.

❏ Never leave a child unattended in the kitchen.

❏ Make sure any sharp knives or other kitchen utensils are out of a child's reach.

❏ Never leave a saucepan handle facing outwards on the cooker top; always make sure they are turned towards the wall, out of reach of little hands.

❏ Never leave your child unattended in the bath, even in a tiny amount of water.

❏ Always make sure your toilet seat is down to avoid a child leaning over and falling in.

MAKE DO AND MEND

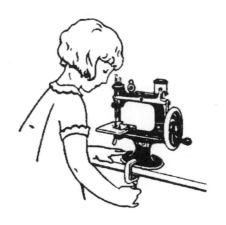

Looking Good on Less

'Make do and mend' was a familiar phrase during wartime in Britain when there was rationing and very little money to spend on anything other than essentials. Many years later, this concept of repairing clothing or making them look like new with accessories is making a come-back. The recent recession has once again made people pull in their financial belts and, rather than go without, they have taken tips from some of the fashion gurus of today and set to altering, mending and embellishing old clothes to give them a new lease of life.

Why not tap into your creative side and start making stylish and original outfits? A new collar, a snazzy belt, a shorter hemline, a bow, new buttons or perhaps a pocket here or there – just a few suggestions to get you started.

You don't need to limit yourself to clothes, of course; sheets, towels, tablecloths, napkins and cushion covers can all be revived with just a few simple stitches.

And don't leave that repair to the last minute, remember the time-honoured phrase, 'A stitch in time saves nine!' There is no need to throw something away just because there is a small hole or stain on it; be creative and cover the patch with a decorative motif, a pocket, a bow or something similar.

If your pennies are really short, why not visit a charity shop and find something you like. A few adjustments can quickly turn the garment into something really special.

I would like to start by teaching beginners the basic sewing stitches and where to use them.

Running stitch is the most basic of all and is made of up and down stitches of equal length and will probably be the one you use the most. This stitch is used to sew seams, to gather fabric, for putting in decorative rows and in quilting.

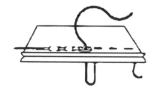

Basting stitch is very similar to running stitch, but it is made with much longer stitches and is usually sewn without knotting the thread so that it is easier to remove. The basting stitch is designed to hold two pieces of fabric together so that the fabric does not move about while you make more permanent stitches.

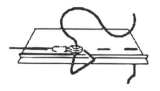

Hemming stitch, as the name implies, is for sewing hems so that as little as possible of the thread is visible on the outside. Start by stitching inside the piece of fabric that is folded down and then take just a few threads from the outer fabric, bringing the needle back up through the edge of the fold.

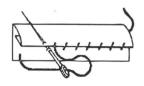

Slip stitch is another type of hemming stitch. It is made by bringing the needle out from the fold of the hem, hiding the knotted end and

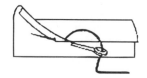

then picking up a few threads of the outside fabric. Stick the needle into the fold and slide it along the inside, bring the needle back out and continue along the hem in this way.

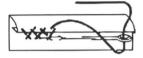

Herringbone stitch is a secure stitch which can be used to sew hems or on projects where you need to attach something securely. Make it by working a diagonal stitch from left to right across the fold, turn the needle to the left and bring the needle out and up towards the right to the folded fabric forming an 'X' with the thread. With the needle still turned to the left, make a small stitch in the fabric from right to left. Continue making sure you cross over the previous stitch to form the 'X'.

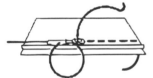

Backstitch is the strongest of the hand stitches and is designed to imitate those created by a sewing machine. Bring the needle up from the back of the fabric and make a backward stitch towards the right. Bring the needle back up to the left, leaving a space between where the needle comes up and the beginning of the last stitch.

Overcast stitch is an invaluable way of stopping fabric from fraying. It is achieved by making diagonal stitches over the raw edge of the fabric. Make sure the stitches are the same length and equally spaced.

Invisible stitch is designed to join two pieces of
fabric together without the stitches showing,
such as for the lining in a skirt or dress. Take
a few threads from the top fabric and then
another few from the bottom fabric.

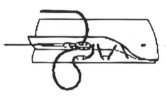

Blanket stitch is used to make a decorative
edging to fabric or for sewing buttonholes.
You can sew this stitch in either direction
by holding the thread along the top edge
of the material with the end pointing in the
direction you are going to sew. Make a loop,
with the top of the loop pointing upwards.
Insert the needle into the loop, then into
the fabric from the wrong side and then
through the large loop left on the right side
of the material. Tighten the stitch and, using
your fingernail, keep the loop on the edge
of the fabric.

Satin stitch is great if you want to embroider
motifs on to a piece of fabric for decoration.
They are flat stitches which are worked very
closely together and can be embroidered
in any direction. Try to keep the stitches as
uniform as possible and work by carrying
the thread across the shape to be filled, then
return the needle underneath the fabric close
to the point where it emerged. Satin stitch is
often made with embroidery thread, which
has less twist than standard sewing thread.

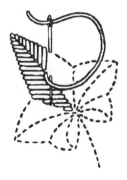

LEARNING HOW TO DARN

Darning can be invaluable if you have a hole in a piece of fabric. The aim is to try and recreate the weave of the fabric so that the darn is as invisible as possible. Try to catch the hole before it gets too large. Darning is great for repairing socks, especially if you have one that is still in good condition. The instructions below are for darning socks, but the same applies if you have a hole in any type of fabric, as long as you choose a thread that matches the cloth rather than wool. In the old days, many women used to have a special tool called a 'mushroom' which they placed inside the sock before darning, but any object with a round end will work just as well.

* Firstly, find a thread or yarn that matches the sock in both colour and texture and then thread a darning needle.
* Place an object with a round end inside the sock and position the hole at the top and pull the fabric taut.
* Start your stitches on either side of the hole by taking several small vertical running stitches in the intact fabric of the sock. Turn the sock upside down and make another row of stitches next to the first. See the diagram, below left, to help you.
* As you get closer to the hole, you should start to increase the number of running stitches you are making. When you reach the point where the hole starts, your stitching line should extend approximately 1 cm (½ in) above and below the hole.
* Continue making vertical running stitches across the area, forming a sort of bridge over the top of the hole.

❋ Once the hole is completely covered, cut the thread and turn your work so that you are working across the original set of stitches. Make running stitches on either side of the hole, but on the stitches that cover the hole weave your needle under and over the vertical threads. Continue stitching back and forth until you have completely filled the hole. Trim off any excess thread and your sock is now ready to be worn without any 'spuds' for your toe to poke through.

USING PATCHES TO COVER HOLES AND TEARS

Patches can be used to cover a multitude of sins – for example, to hide stains, holes, tears or areas that have been worn away by knobbly knees or elbows. The secret is to find a piece of fabric that is as close to the original as possible.

If the garment has a pocket on it, you could consider sewing the pocket up permanently and using a piece of fabric from underneath. It is possible to buy iron-on patches which, although they are easy to use, I find always come off after a couple of washes.

Make sure you keep a plentiful supply of old pieces of fabric, particularly offcuts from old denim jeans, as these always come in handy for making patches or for appliqué work if you want to be more adventurous.

❋ Cut out a patch which is at least 1 cm (½ in) larger than the hole you wish to cover.

❋ Pin the patch over the top of the hole, making sure that the hole is in the centre and that the patch is the right side up.

❋ You can either set your sewing machine to do a zig-zag stitch or you can sew the patch in place by hand using one of the stitches recommended on pages 87 to 89.

SEWING A HEM

Ideally the sewing on a hem should be practically invisible from the outside of the garment. A badly stitched or uneven hem can ruin the appearance of your outfit, so make sure you take the time to get it right. It is important to mark where you want the finished hem to be before sewing, and this can be done either by pinning or marking with some tailor's chalk. Follow these simple guidelines:

* Put on the item you wish to hem, making sure you are wearing the correct shoes you would like to go with the outfit.
* Stand on a box or a chair and ask someone to mark where you want the hemline to be. They can either place a couple of pins or alternatively mark with some tailor's chalk.
* Now remove the item and, using a tape measure, mark or pin the hem all the way round to the desired length, allowing a minimum of 2.5 cm (1 in) for the fold. Do not leave the fold too wide, otherwise the hem will not sit flat, especially if the item is flared.
* If the fabric is liable to fray and you have cut the item to make it shorter, you will first need to oversew the edges.
* Now neatly sew around the hem, using your very best hemming stitch.

REPLACING WORN-OUT COLLARS AND CUFFS

It is usually the areas that come into contact with the skin that wear out first on a shirt. Rather than just throwing it in the bin, why not have a go at replacing the collars and cuffs, either with the same fabric or with a contrasting one to make it look completely different.

* Using a seam ripper, remove the stitching between the cuffs and the sleeve ends. Do the same with the collar.

✻ Now unfold the cuffs and collar and find the stitching that attaches them to the body of the shirt. Carefully remove the stitching with your seam ripper.

✻ Turn the cuffs and collar inside out and take apart the side seams. Make sure you mark the fabric on the edge which attaches to the garment.

✻ Now iron the old cuffs and collar so that they are completely flat. Lay out your new piece of fabric and pin the old collar and cuffs to it to form a pattern. Remember to allow a 0.6 cm (¼ in) seam allowance all round. Cut around the pattern pieces so that you now have four new pieces.

✻ Unpin the old collar and cuffs and fold under one of the bottom edges of the collar pieces and iron it flat.

✻ Place the new collar pieces together so that the right sides are facing each other. Pin the top and side edges together.

✻ Sew the top and side seams together, making sure you keep the seam allowance. Now turn the collar right side out.

✻ Pin the unfolded bottom edge of the collar to the neck of your shirt, making sure you have the right sides facing each other. Sew the edges together. Pull the folded bottom edge of the collar over the seam allowances and pin it to the line of stitches. Using slipstitch, attach the folded edge to the shirt and then iron the collar flat.

✻ Now take the new cuff pieces and pin the side seam of each one together. Sew the side seams, remembering to allow for your seam allowance. Iron the seams open and flat.

✻ Take each cuff piece and fold it in half with the wrong sides facing each other. Fold under one edge on each cuff and iron the folds flat. Pin the unfolded edges of the cuffs to the ends of the sleeve with the right sides facing each other. Sew the cuffs to the sleeve ends.

❋ Next pull the folded edges of the cuffs over the seam allowance and pin them along the line of stitching. Using slipstitch sew the folded edges to the sleeves. Iron, and hey presto you have a shirt that is as good as new.

MAKE YOUR OWN CROSS STITCH PATCH

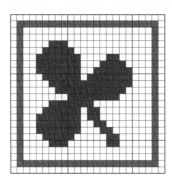

If you have a favourite pair of denim jeans or trousers that now have a hole or a tear in them, you can always embellish them by making your own cross stitch patch to sew over the damaged area. You can draw your own design and simply work out where the stitches go by using some graph paper. The one I am showing you here is to celebrate St Patrick's Day and each coloured square indicates a single cross stitch.

❋ Choose your design. I suggest you start with something simple and not too large. Using graph paper draw the design and then fill in each square that requires a cross stitch.

❋ Now take a piece of felt larger than you want the finished patch to be. Take a piece of open weave canvas and tack it in place on top of the felt.

❋ Carefully following the pattern on your graph paper, embroider your chosen design on to the canvas using embroidery thread in the colour or colours of your choice.

❋ When you have finished your cross stitch design, trim both the canvas and felt to the desired size, leaving the edges of the felt slightly larger so that you can overlap the edges of the canvas.

❋ Sew the felt over the edge of the canvas with an attractive
  embroidery stitch.
❋ Before stitching the patch on to your jeans or other item of
  clothing, I would suggest washing and drying the patch first
  so that you don't risk it shrinking or the colour running when
  it is in place.

A SIMPLE DENIM BAG

This bag is incredibly simple to make and means that your
old jeans have been recycled instead of simply throwing them
away. I made two of these for my grandchildren to use for their
schoolbags; they were a great hit.

❋ Cut a piece of denim 30 x 40 cm (12 x 16 in) from a leg of
  your old jeans, leaving the side seams intact. Fold a 1 cm
  (½ in) strip around the top and sew it down to make a casing
  for some ribbon or cord. Feed the cord or ribbon through the
  casing and then knot the two ends together. This forms the
  main body of the bag.
❋ For the bottom of the bag cut another piece of denim which is
  about 1 cm (½ in) larger than the circumference of the bag.
❋ Turn the bag inside out and pin the bottom piece of the body of
  the bag in place, making sure that the correct sides are touching
  each other. Sew the pieces together.
❋ Now turn the bag the right way out and embellish it by either
  painting with fabric paint, embroidery, decorative patches or
  some pretty buttons.

MAKING A FABRIC BELT

It is easy to dress up an outfit with a snazzy belt, whether
you want to wear it slung low on your hips, or higher up to

accentuate your waistline. By making your own you can get it exactly the right length and also choose the best colour to go with your outfit. The only fitting required is measuring your waist. If an unusual buckle catches your eye when browsing round a boot fair or a charity shop but you don't like the belt, buy it anyway and make your own using the buckle. It is far easier if you remove the prong first, then you won't have to go to the trouble of making holes in your belt.

* Start out by measuring your waist.
* Measure the width of your buckle and then allow an extra 1 cm (½ in) seam allowance for both sides. This will give you the width of your belt.
* Cut out one piece of your chosen fabric to the length of your waist measurement and add about 20 cm (8 in) to allow for overlap.
* Cut a piece of fusable interfacing the same length but slightly narrower than your length of fabric. Now press the raw edges towards the centre of the fabric 1 cm (½ in) on each side.
* I like to back my belt with a piece of grosgrain ribbon, which should be sewn in place 6 cm (2½ in) from one end and 17.5 cm (7 in) from the other.
* On the end with the ribbon 17.5 cm from the end, fold down 1 cm to hide the raw edge and fold the fabric back on to the ribbon. Stitch down both long sides close to the end.

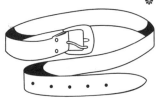

* On the other end fold back 1 cm and fold again 2.5 cm (1 in) over the centre bar of the belt. Stitch in place and you are finished. You could, if you prefer, use D-rings instead of the buckle, or jazz the whole thing up with a decorative bow.

HOW TO MAKE A RIBBON HEADBAND

Headbands make great accessories and by coming up with your own you can save yourself quite a few pennies. The options for decorating these headbands are endless and you can choose exactly what colour you want.

* Take a measurement of the circumference of your head at the level where you intend to wear the band.
* Cut your piece of ribbon about 2.5 cm (1 in) shorter than the measurement of your head.
* Sew a piece of elastic to one end of the ribbon, making sure the elastic is hidden neatly underneath the folded end of the ribbon.
* Before sewing the other end, test that the headband fits round your head snugly and comfortably. Mark the place and sew the elastic to the other end.
* Now you can decorate your headband as you please.

USING UP OLD KNITTING WOOL

If you have an old hand-knitted jumper or other item that is past its sell-by date, or perhaps you are tired of wearing, don't throw it away, simply unpick it and re-use the wool to make something new and useful. You might think a knitted hat would be difficult to do and that it would be worked in a circle. This pattern, however, makes life easy as it is knitted flat and then sewn up afterwards. You will need a fairly big, bulky wool for this pattern but it is easy and quick to put together and makes a great present for Christmas.

You will need:
approx. 31 m (34 yds) bulky knitting wool

1 pair 19 (1 mm) knitting needles
scissors
1 darning needle

Gauge:
one and a half stiches and two rows per 2.5 cm (1 in) in
garter stitch.

Finished size:
The finished hat is about 22.5 cm (9 in) tall and 38 cm (15 in)
in circumference. This should stretch to fit an average-sized
woman's head.

Instructions:
* Cast on 15 stitches.
* Knit every row until the piece measures 38 cm (15 in).
* Cast off and cut the wool.
* Sew the cast-on edge to the cast-off edge.
* Thread some wool through the stitches along one of the sides
  of the tube. Pull tightly so that there is no hole in the end.
  Now thread the wool back through the stitches to make sure
  it is firmly secured. Cut the wool.
* Finish off by weaving in any unsightly ends.

EMBELLISHING OLD SHOES

Are your young ones bored with their old trainers but have not
outgrown them yet? Rather than throw them away, why not
suggest to them that they decorate them in some way to bring
them back to life. You could suggest that, instead of laces, they
put a brightly coloured ribbon in their place. Alternatively, if
they are really creative they could draw patterns on the rubber

toe. Another way is to divide the shoe up into sections, apply some fabric glue to each section and then sprinkle on some multi-coloured glitter. Buckles and bows stitched or stuck on the front can also make the shoes look quite different and stylish. Of course, these suggestions are for girls; I can't see boys going for any such thing.

Flip-flops are also easy to decorate and fun for kids. You can glue sequins, small beads or even some glitter on to the Y-shaped straps. You could also glue stars or tiny metallic stickers round the sides or wind some coloured ribbon round the Y-shaped straps to make them look more attractive. Plastic flowers glued on the front look pretty, or multi-coloured feathers make them look really different. You could also ask your children to come up with a few innovative ideas.

RECYCLING THAT OLD T-SHIRT

Making things out of old T-shirts is entertaining and costs very little, just like this fun bracelet.

* Cut long rectangles out of some old T-shirt material, approximately 1 cm (½ in) wide and a little bigger than the circumference of your wrist. You can use three or four strips if you know how to plait with four pieces.
* Line up your strands, pin them together at the top to hold them in place and then start plaiting. Plait until you reach the end. If you like you can add some beads or charms as you go.
* Take the ends and lay them on top of one another, then sew together to form a circle.

WASTE NOT
WANT NOT

Changing Your Living Habits

Learning how to change the way you live your life isn't nearly as difficult as it might sound and, in truth, you will only be reverting to a way of life that my generation took for granted. These days, we are all being encouraged to 'go green' or become more 'eco-friendly', modern jargon for trying to waste less and cause less pollution to our planet. I am afraid I still don't fully understand all the implications of 'global warming', but I do know that if we can encourage our children and grandchildren to stop and think about the things they care about, then maybe we can have a beneficial impact for future generations.

I am not talking about major changes, just simple things like learning to recycle, walking or riding a bike instead of always using the car and remembering to turn off a light or an appliance when not using it. My generation did not have the money to go wasting anything, so I am hoping that, by returning to the standards of bygone days, my own household can now become at least a little bit 'greener'.

RECYCLING
If you are not already recycling, then it is important to know why this can really make a difference. When we recycle an item, it means that the material it is made out of is converted into a new product. This means that the manufacturers need to use less natural, raw material from our planet. It is vitally important

that we try to conserve our natural resources, especially when thousands of acres of natural forest are being destroyed each year to meet our demands. This is not only damaging the environment, it also endangers many species of wildlife, some of which will become extinct.

Manufacturing using recycled materials also consumes less energy than that needed for producing products from new materials. Not only does it require less transportation, but the extraction and refinement process required to prepare the raw material for manufacture also means less energy is required.

If we can recycle as much as possible of our household waste, it means the amount of rubbish sent to landfill sites will be greatly reduced. I am not sure exactly how many landfill sites there are currently in operation, but I do know that these sites produce a quarter of the country's emissions of methane. Methane is the powerful greenhouse gas which is doing the most damage to our environment.

WHAT CAN OR CAN'T BE RECYCLED?
Aerosols
Most recycling centres will take aerosols provided they are not crushed, pierced or flattened.

Asbestos
Asbestos must only be removed by a professional as it can be very harmful. However, it can be recycled and many councils will accept it at their centres.

Books
Believe it or not books cannot be recycled

because of the glue that is used to bind them together. The best way to dispose of books is to donate them to a charity shop or school. Some hospitals and hospices are also able to accept second-hand books.

Batteries
Batteries need to be disposed of carefully so if you cannot find a battery recycling option, contact the manufacturer for further instructions. When it is time to change your batteries, consider buying rechargeable ones instead.

It is forbidden by law to dispose of car batteries with household waste. You will find many garages or scrap metal facilities will take these for you.

Building materials
Most building materials such as bricks and wood can be reused. Others such as glass, plastic or metal can be recycled either at your local centre or at a salvage yard.

Cars
Cars are a good source of recyclable materials, so find out from your local authority where you can take your old one.

Clothing
Most recycling centres have separate bins for clothing. Alternatively, take them to a charity shop or a shelter for homeless people who will make good use of them.

Computers, cameras and elecrical goods
If your television, computer or camera is still in working

order you might like to consider donating it to charity. Otherwise any electrical equipment has to be disposed of at a professional waste disposal facility and you are supposed to keep proof that you have disposed of any electrical goods by the correct channel.

Glasses

Unwanted glasses or spectacles can be accepted at local recycling centres, but there are many schools, religious organizations and charities who could make better use of them.

Glass

Glass is usually sorted into three colours at recycling centres – green, brown and clear and you should make sure they are clean and any corks or tops removed before disposing of them.

Metal

Metal is divided into two separate groups: steel and aluminium. If you are not sure which type of metal you are getting rid of, you can test it with a magnet – steel will attract the magnet, while aluminium will not. Most recycling centres have separate bins for old drinks cans or you may have a 'Cash for cans' scheme in operation in your district.

Mobile phones

Before throwing your old phone in the bin, consider that 80 per cent of it is recyclable. It is better to return it to the shop where it was bought, or look out for any charities or organizations that will accept them for refurbishment. Some supermarkets are also able to take mobile phones for recycling.

Paint

Paint can't really be recycled but it shouldn't be wasted, so make sure you seal the can properly when you have finished with it to stop it from drying out. You can take it to your local recycling centre who should have a donation point for paint, or you can give it to a local community repainting scheme.

Paper

All kinds of paper can be recycled and it is usually divided into separate categories at the local recycling centre: newspapers, magazines, cardboard, office paper etc. Even the Yellow Pages directory can be recycled these days. Avoid shredding paper unless it contains private details, as many authorities are unable to take it in this form and many of the processing plants are unable to handle shredded paper.

When you next buy stationery, why not consider buying paper that has already been recycled.

Plastic

There are over 50 different types of plastic and almost all of these can be accepted by recycling centres. Make sure any detergent bottles are washed clean and preferably pressed flat.

Printer cartridges

There are not many places that will accept printer cartridges, but often charities and schools collect these items for recycling.

Use it Wisely

WATER

Water is a valuable resource and I don't think it was until
I experienced my first hosepipe ban not so long ago that I
actually learned how to use it wisely. I made a list which I stuck
to the refrigerator door and asked everyone if they could please
save as much water as possible. If you have a water meter,
you will quickly notice a difference; even if you don't you are
helping to conserve something that is often in short supply.
Here are a few things you can do to save water at home:

* Please don't leave the tap running while washing the dishes.
  Fill a separate sink or bowl with rinsing water.
* Only run the washing machine and dishwasher when they
  have a full load.
* Use a jug of cold water in the refrigerator rather than running
  the tap for drinks.
* Only water the garden in the morning or evening when the
  temperatures are cooler.
* Take a shower instead of a bath and shorten the length of time
  you spend in it by one or two minutes.
* Save the water from your shower, bath or fish tank and use it
  for watering the garden.
* Reduce the tap flow to a trickle when shaving or brushing
  your teeth.
* Either buy something like the Hippo Water Saver, a tough
  water-filled polythene bag, or fill a couple of quart-sized

plastic bottles with small stones and place them on the opposite side to the handle in the toilet cystern. This means that your toilet will not use as much water each time you flush.

* Install a couple of water butts to collect water from your roof to water your garden.
* Make sure you fix a leaky tap immediately as this can waste a lot of water.
* Teach your children to turn off taps when they have finished at the sink.
* Use a layer of organic mulch on the surface of your planting beds to minimize water loss.
* If you use a carwash, make sure it is one that recycles its water.
* Bathe your dogs outside on a nice sunny day – that way, the lawn will get a watering too.

CONSERVING ENERGY

As the cost of living continues to rise at an alarming rate, there has never been a better time to start saving energy. Even small changes can help save you money and have less of a detrimental impact on our environment. Start today by trying a few of these energy-saving tips:

* Replace all your old light bulbs with energy-efficient ones. Although they will cost you more initially, the saving in the long run will be very beneficial.
* Make sure you turn off all electrical devices that are not in use. Even leaving devices on stand-by can use quite a considerable amount of electricity.
* Make sure you put weather-proof strips round all your windows and doors if you do not have double-glazing.

* Turn your refrigerator down a couple of degrees and make
  sure that its energy-saver switch is on.
* Only wash your clothes on a warm or cold water setting.
  Believe it or not, cold water does still get them clean.
* If you can turn off the drying cycle on your
  dishwasher, do so. Just leave the dishes to dry
  naturally in the air. The heat from the wash cycle will
  be enough for them to dry quickly.
* Turn down the thermostat on your heating by a notch
  or two.
* Turn down the thermostat on your water heater too.
* If you need to replace any electrical appliance, make
  sure you choose models that have energy-efficient
  labels on them.
* If you have air-conditioning in your home, make sure you
  replace or clean the air filters regularly.
* Make sure your hot water tank is properly insulated.
* Use less hot water by installing low-flow shower heads.
* Make sure your loft is properly insulated.
* If possible, dry your clothes outdoors rather than using a
  tumble dryer.

You might like to look into what grants are available in your
area, for things like wall cavity insulation, or upgrading your
central heating boiler to a more efficient type. This is certainly
worth considering as it will save you a considerable amount
of money in the long run. It is estimated that as much as 27
per cent of carbon emissions are generated by our own homes,
so any improvements you make can have a lasting impact on
cutting down this figure.

Using up Leftovers

I was raised to be frugal, to use every scrap of food that we had in the house, so I find it difficult to come to terms with the amount of food we waste. Just think how much money you could save by careful planning and only buying what you need. With a couple of extra ingredients and a little imagination, it is possible to turn almost any leftovers into great tasting meals.

Here are some some suggestions for the more common leftover ingredients that you probably have in your kitchen right now. Don't just dump them, give some of these ideas a try and you will be amazed how popular they will become with your family. Also consider cutting down on the size of your portions if you are regularly scraping food from the plates into the bin. Your family can always ask for more if they feel they haven't eaten enough.

THINGS TO DO WITH STALE BREAD
You have half a loaf of bread in your breadbin which is starting to go stale. There is no need to throw this out for the birds. Try one of the following – they really are delicious.
* Bread stuffing for poultry or pork
* Bread and butter pudding
* Mini pizzas – all you need to do is cut circles out of some slices of bread and toast on one side. In a food processor mix some cherry tomatoes, tomato purée, a few herbs and a tsp of sugar and process until you have a paste. Spread on top of the

bread circles, top with grated cheese and then brown under the grill. These are delicious and your kids will love them.

* Croutons to go on top of some homemade soup
* French toast

USING UP COOKED RICE

I don't know about you but I always seem to cook too much rice. There is no need to throw this away, put it in a container in the fridge and the following day make one of the following:

* Special fried rice
* Sweet rice and raisin pudding
* Spanish paella
* Mushroom risotto
* Vegetable pilaff

BANANAS

These days people don't seem to like brown bananas, as the supermarkets only seem to sell yellow ones that are under-ripe. Even if you don't like a nice, sweet, ripe banana, there is no need to throw them out as soon as the skin gets a little brown. Try one of these:

* Banana bread
* Banana milkshake
* Banana and fruit smoothie
* Banana muffins
* Banana and sourmilk pancakes

VEGETABLES

If you have some vegetables left over after, say, a Sunday roast, keep them and make one of the following:

* Spicy vegetable curry
* Vegetable soup
* Quick stir-fry
* Roasted to go with some chops the following day
* Bubble and squeak

CHICKEN
Chicken is quite safe to cook for a second time as long as you make sure it is thoroughly heated all the way through.
* Chicken noodle soup
* Chicken stir-fry
* Spicy chicken burgers
* Chicken soup
* Chicken and leek pie
* Cold with salad

LAMB OR BEEF
Leftover lamb or beef can be minced and made into either shepherds pie or cottage pie.
* Curry
* Stir-fry
* Moussaka
* Spicy lamb kebabs
* Cold with salad

FISH
* Fishcakes
* Fish pie
* Quick Spanish paella

❋ Fish and pasta bake
❋ Fish goujons
❋ Fish pâté

EGGS

❋ If you have an abundance of eggs to use up as they are coming up to the sell-by date, I suggest you make a yummy Spanish tortilla omelette. This will not only use a lot of eggs but you can put some of those leftover vegetables in it too.
❋ Pancakes are also good for using up eggs and make a wonderful and quick dessert. You can put any fruit with them and then add a drizzle of honey for sweetness.
❋ Finally, why not have a good dollop of scrambled eggs on toast with breakfast or, for a really indulgent one, add some smoked salmon.

I couldn't resist adding my recipe for carrot cake, which not only uses four eggs but cooked carrots, ripe pineapple and any leftover cottage cheese as well. It is very moist and has been a hit with my family for years.

THE VERY BEST CARROT CAKE

Ingredients
   225 g (8 oz) self-raising flour
   ½ tsp salt
   ½ tsp ground cinnamon
   ½ tsp bicarbonate of soda
   4 eggs

225 g (8 oz) soft brown sugar
½ tsp vanilla essence
100 g (3.5 oz) cooked carrot, finely chopped
75 g (2.5 oz) ripe pineapple, puréed
75 g (2.5 oz) walnuts
75 g (2.5 oz) dessicated coconut
125 ml (4 fl oz) sunflower oil

For the topping
75 g (2.5 oz) cream or cottage cheese
1 tsp vanilla essence
175 g (6 oz) icing sugar

Method
* Preheat the oven to 180°C/350°F/gas mark 4. Grease and line the base of a 20 cm (8 in) round cake tin with greased baking parchment.
* Sift the flour, salt, cinnamon and bicarbonate of soda into a large bowl. Beat together the eggs, sugar, vanilla essence, carrot, pineapple, walnuts, coconut and oil.
* Make a well in the centre of the flour and pour in the wet ingredients and mix well until combined.
* Spoon the mixture into the prepared tin and bake for 45 to 50 minutes or until a cake tester comes out clean. Leave in the tin to cool for about 10 minutes before turning out.
* To make the icing, beat together the cream or cottage cheese with the vanilla essence and icing sugar until it is smooth. Spoon the icing over the top of the cake and spread with a pallet knife. It doesn't need to be too smooth; a rough effect actually looks better.

Making Toys from Salvaged Materials

It seems to me that children today have an abundance of toys, many of which are discarded after just a few hours of playing. As a child I know I always had more fun with the box that the toy came in than the toy itself, often turning it into a miniature puppet theatre, a shop or, if it was large enough, a boat which I pretended was a pirate ship.

Why not have a go at making some toys from used household items that would otherwise end up in the bin. Not only is it an economical way to replenish the toy box, it ought to help to stimulate your child's imagination as they can help you with the project.

* Save your old plastic bottles to make an indoor bowling alley. For added fun, you can get your children to decorate them. Line them up like the skittles at a bowling alley and then use a tennis ball to try and knock them down.
* Shops was one of my favourite games as a child so don't throw away empty cereal boxes, soap bottles, coffee jars or juice containers, just rinse them out and keep them for a shop. Give your child some old buttons to use as money.
* Make your own jigsaw puzzles by first asking your child to choose a favourite picture out of an old comic or magazine, or alternatively getting them to draw or paint a picture of their own. Glue the picture on to a piece of cardboard and leave it

until it is thoroughly dry. Now cut the picture into several pieces, jumble them up and ask your child to reassemble them. This can be really good fun if you do this with a friend and see if you can do each other's puzzle.

* Make a puppet theatre. Children love playing with puppets and making up their own theatrical shows. You will need a cardboard box that is large enough for two children to fit behind when they perform the show. Cut a large opening in the front of the box. Attach a piece of string across the opening at the top and then thread two pieces of fabric along it to make the curtain. You will also need to make two holes in the back to allow the children to get their hands through. Get your child to paint some scenery on the inside of the box. Make some puppets by using some old brightly coloured socks. Use buttons to make the faces, or paint some on using fabric paint. Now ask the children to slip the puppets over their hands and then sit back and enjoy their show. I guarantee you will have some laughs.

* For the boys you can make a garage out of an old shoebox to hold their cars. You can divide it into different sections with pieces of cardboard.

* For the girls make a dolls house out of a large cardboard box, or several smaller ones glued together. Divide it into separate rooms and then get your child to help you decorate the room with old pieces of wallpaper or fabric. You can also make tiny pieces of furniture using matchsticks and old matchboxes. This will really bring out the creative side in your children.

* Fishing is another game my children loved and it is very easy to make. The only thing you will need to buy is a set of tiny magnets. Get a large cardboard box and position it so that the opening is at the top. Get your children to paint the inside so

that it looks like water. Now get them to draw some fish on pieces of cardboard and paint them with bright colours. On the end of each fish glue one of the magnets and allow to dry thoroughly. Now making some fishing rods out of pieces of dowel or perhaps some short pieces of garden cane. Attach a piece of string to one end and then attach a magnet to the end of the string. Make sure you have magnets that attract each other on the fish and the rod. Place the fish in the bottom of the box, get your children to kneel at the side and then set the children a time limit. The one that catches the most fish in that time is the winner.

* Hoopla is another old-fashioned game that is always a winner with kids. Save your old fizzy drinks bottles and then weight them down by putting stones in the bottom. Make some hoops out of old cardboard that are large enough to go over the whole bottle. Get your children to paint them different colours and allow them to dry. Using a different colour for each child, ask them to try and throw the hoops over the bottles. The one that gets the most hits is the winner.

* Another fishy game we used to play at home was fish racing. Again, get your children to draw some fairly large fish on pieces of paper and then colour them in with bright colours. Mark out some lanes on the floor using some old string and then place a piece at the end which will mark the finishing line. Now lay the fish out in a row at the start of each lane. Give the children an old newspaper that has been folded in half and get them to flap the paper as hard as possible directly behind each fish. The one that manages to stay in his lane and reaches the finishing line first is the winner.

IN THE GARDEN

The 'No Dig' Garden

Growing your own fruit and veg is a wonderful, fulfilling way of making sure you eat delicious, fresh, healthy food and save money into the bargain. And it's easy if you follow the 'No Dig' method. This consists of a raised bed that has been filled with different layers of organic matter. With this method it doesn't matter what type of soil you have in your area, because you will be providing your own rich compost. Raised beds are exceptionally easy to build, once established they are virtually maintenance-free and you can build them anywhere as long as it is sheltered and gets plenty of sun. Also, an added bonus, especially as you get older, is that there is not as much bending.

HOW TO START A NO DIG GARDEN

The first thing to do is to choose the site for your garden, bearing in mind that it will need to get at least four hours of sun a day. The ground should be level, so make sure you get rid of any humps and bumps. Mark out the area and then decide what sort of border you want to use – bricks, wood or some type of solid fencing – and then form the area in which you wish to build up your compost. In a perfect world, the border should be no less than 25 cm (10 in) in height. Ideally, only make your garden twice as wide as you can reach, then you can reach the middle without having to walk on the plot.

The first layer should be newspaper. This can either be

shredded or laid down in sheets directly on top of the soil so that it is at least 5 mm (¼ in) thick.

Your next layer should be alfalfa to a depth of about 10 cm (4 in) and on top of that a good organic fertilizer, such as well-rotted horse, cow or sheep manure, or even garden compost, to a depth of 20 mm (1 in). On top of this add a thick layer of loosely laid straw to a depth of 20 cm (8 in) topped with another layer of fertilizer. The final layer should be a good-quality compost to a depth of 10 cm (4 in).

Now water well until all the layers are damp but not soaking wet and you are ready to start planting your seedlings.

PLANTING YOUR NO DIG GARDEN
A No Dig garden works much better if you use seedlings rather than seeds and, because the soil is so rich, you can plant more intensively than you would in a regular garden. Divide your bed up into rows, which you can mark with pieces of string or whatever method you choose. Once you have decided what is going where, plant your seedlings and then cover any exposed area with a layer of mulch to keep the moisture in and the weeds out. Try not to get the mulch too close to the stems of your seedlings, though, because this can encourage stem rot.

If you are new to gardening, then start small and add to the bed as your confidence grows. Remember to allow space for some companion planting, as this will not only bring some colour to your plot but it will discourage many pests.

Remember to rotate your crops so that you can take full advantage of the growing season. The secret to success is planning in advance and learning the secrets of using crop rotation, which is explained over the page.

THE ADVANTAGES OF CROP ROTATION

The reason we need to learn the art of crop rotation is because different plants take different nutrients out of the soil while others add them back into the mix. If you don't want your soil to become tired each season, crops need to be rotated. This means not growing the same vegetable in the same spot year after year. Of course, this does not apply to perennial plants such as asparagus, which remain in the same place all the time.

Start by dividing your plot into different sections, four for smaller beds or eight for those with a larger plot. Although I cannot predict which vegetables you will choose to grow, I will give an example of rotating the crop systematically around the raised bed. Make sure you keep a written record of what you plant and where. Below is an example of a typical four-bed and six-bed rotation:

Bed 1 – Onions and other root crops
Bed 2 – Peas, beans and brassicas
Bed 3 – Tomatoes, aubergines and peppers
Bed 4 – Sweecorn, cucumbers and squashes

Bed 1 – Peas and beans
Bed 2 – Brassicas (broccoli, cauliflower,
            cabbage, Brussels sprouts)
Bed 3 – Root crops (carrots, parsnips, potatoes)
Bed 4 – Sweetcorn and cucumbers
Bed 5 – Tomatoes, aubergines and peppers
Bed 6 – Green manure crop

Rotation is also important in preventing pests and disease gaining a foothold.

GUIDE TO PLANTING OUT AND HARVESTING

Without going into too much detail, I am including a rough guide to planting out your seedlings and when you can expect to harvest them. Of course, this will vary according to where you live and how harsh your seasons are, so make sure you adjust your growing according to the weather in your area. Remember, when it comes to harvesting from a No Dig bed, the idea is to disturb the soil as little as possible. Most root vegetables can be gently pulled up, but areas that have been disturbed should be replenished with mulch as quickly as possible. Even with the No Dig method, it is inevitable that the soil will be turned over, but it is a lot less than conventional digging, so the condition of the soil does not deteriorate as much.

March planting

* March is the month when things really start to grow as the soil is beginning to warm up. You can help it along by pegging some horticultural fleece over your raised garden for a week or so before you intend to plant. You will be surprised what a difference it makes.
* As long as it is not too wet, you can plant your onion and shallot sets which should go in about 30 cm (12 in) apart.
* Mid March is the time to establish an asparagus bed, and for this you will have to do a bit of digging in your No Dig garden, as it will require a trench about 15 cm (6 in) deep. Although asparagus will take a few years to establish, you can rely on approximately 25 years of produce from your original crowns.
* You can start planting your early potatoes that you have had chitting in the shed in mid-March. Plant them in a

trench about 20 cm (8 in) deep and 75 cm (29 in) apart.
* You can also plant Jerusalem artichoke tubers this month.

March harvesting
* Any leeks and parsnips that are still in the ground should be dug up now.
* You may also have some late Brussels sprouts, winter cauliflowers, kale and swedes.

April planting
* April is a great month for gardeners because the soil is really warming up, but remember to keep an eye on the weather forecast as you don't want to be caught out by frosts.
* If you haven't already planted them, globe and Jerusalem artichokes, onion and shallot sets and asparagus can all be planted this month.
* Strawberries can be planted out this month, but if you are planting them for the first time it is a good idea to pinch out the flowers in the first year because this will give the plants added strength and give you an improved crop the following year. Strawberry plants do not last forever, so you will need to rotate them every three to five years.
* Other things you can sow this month are: beetroot, peas, broad beans, broccoli, Brussels sprouts, cabbage, cauliflower, kale, chard, kohl rabi, leeks, spinach, rocket, lettuce and radishes.

April harvesting
* April is a lean month for harvesting, so you will just have to be patient.

May planting

* May is probably one of the busiest months for the gardener as everything starts to grow well this month.
* There are many things to sow this month: French beans, runner beans, beetroot, broccoli, cabbage, cauliflower, chicory, kale, kohl rabi, peas, turnips, swedes, salad leaves (in succession), radishes and spring onions.
* You can plant out Brussels sprouts, summer cabbage, celery, celeriac, leeks, aubergine, peppers, cucumber and tomatoes.

May harvesting

* You may well have hardy lettuce, spring onions and fast-growing radishes ready for harvesting.
* If your asparagus bed is well established, you may find this is now starting to crop.

June planting

* June should be really warming up now and you will be starting to reap the rewards of your hard work.
* There are plenty of things you can sow this month. It is possible to sow one set now and then a few weeks later sow again, to give you a succession of fresh vegetables throughout the season. Sow French and runner beans, maincrop peas, beetroot, carrots, turnips, swedes, cauliflowers, chicory, kohl rabi, sweetcorn, squash, courgettes and marrows and cucumbers.
* You can now plant out brassicas such as broccoli, Brussels sprouts and summer cabbage.
* Tumbling tomatoes are easy to grow in pots as they do not grow tall and will not require pinching out.

❊ Watch out for the eggs of butterflies on the undersides of brassicas as they will hatch into caterpillars which can soon make a meal of your crop.

June harvesting
❊ Salad crops should be available – lettuce, spring onions, radishes etc. Summer cabbage and early carrots. Early potatoes should be ready this month, as well as beetroot, young turnips and summer spinach.

July planting
❊ Much of this month will be spent watering, but a layer of organic mulch on the surface of your bed should help to keep the moisture in. However, you will need to keep on top of the slugs as they will love the damp conditions.
❊ There are still a few crops you can sow this month – spring cabbage, chicory, kohl rabi, lettuce, peas, French beans, beetroot, carrots and radishes.
❊ If you have not already done it, now is the time to plant out your leeks. Make a hole about 15 cm (6 in) deep and drop the leek directly into the hole and make sure it is well watered.

July harvesting
❊ Your harvest will be abundant this month and should provide you with broad, French and runner beans, beetroot, cabbage, cauliflowers and broccoli, carrots, celery, courgettes, cucumbers, kale, kohl rabi, lettuce, onions, spring onions, peas, early potatoes, radishes, spinach, tomatoes and turnips. When harvesting your potatoes, make sure you dig the ground well to ensure you have removed all the tubers.

❈ Keep on top of aphids (particularly on the tips of broad beans) by washing them off the plants with a strong jet of water, or spray with a solution of soft soap and water. This will not damage the plants and hopefully will reduce the numbers. I would advise planting some African marigolds among your vegetables as they are well known to be the perfect companion plant. They exude chemicals from their roots that help to repel pests from neighbouring plants.

August planting

❈ You can still sow spring cabbage, kohl rabi, lettuce (winter hardy), spring onions (winter hardy), radishes, spinach and turnips.
❈ Savoy cabbages, cauliflowers and kale can all be planted out this month.

August harvesting

❈ Many crops will be ready to harvest this month, including lettuce, onions, spring onions, peas, early maincrop potatoes, radishes, spinach, tomatoes, turnips, French beans, runner beans, cabbage, carrots, cauliflower, celery, courgettes, cucumbers, kale and kohl rabi.

September planting

❈ There is not much to sow this time of year except perhaps a winter lettuce for spring harvest.
❈ You can plant out spring cabbages and Japanese onions sets can go in for an early harvest.

September harvesting

* There are still plenty of crops to harvest this month including beetroot, cabbage, carrots, cauliflowers, courgettes, cucumbers, globe artichokes, kale, kohl rabi, lettuce, leeks, marrows, onions, squashes, radishes, spring onions, spinach, sweetcorn, tomatoes and turnips.
* Maincrop potatoes should be ready for harvesting now. A little tip when digging up your potatoes is to harvest them early in the day and leave them in the sunlight for a day so that the skins harden off before storing. That way there is less risk of damage. Do not put any damaged potatoes in your sacks as they will quickly rot and damage the rest of the potatoes.
* You might find you still have a few peas and French beans left, but the main crop will have finished.

October planting

* This is the month to start collecting leaves as they are a valuable resource for making leaf mould. Build yourself a cage by driving four stakes into the ground and stapling some chicken wire around them. Just throw the leaves in there and leave for a year.
* You can still plant out Japanese onions although you might well need to cover them with some fleece to give them a good start.
* You can plant your garlic now, although you can wait until November if you prefer.
* This is the month that you can split and plant rhubarb crowns.
* You can also sow a hardy winter lettuce which will give you some salad leaves whatever the weather decides to do.

October harvesting

* The last of your maincrop potatoes should now be ready. Carrots can also come up and be stored in sand.
* Leave the parsnips in the ground as the flavour improves after a frost.
* Cabbages should come up now and they will keep well if you have a shed that is sheltered from frost.
* If you have any green tomatoes left on your tomato plants, you may as well pick them now before they are destroyed by frost. You can ripen them indoors or make a wonderful green tomato chutney – see recipe on page 131.

November planting

* This is the time to plant your garlic as it actually benefits from the cold weather.

November harvesting

* By now the hard frosts have usually started, so I would suggest bringing in your winter cabbages and cauliflowers. You should also have some Brussels sprouts ready – there is no need to wait until Christmas!
* You should find some of your leeks are ready for harvesting, but only take as much as you need as the rest can stay in the ground.
* Other things that could still be available are celery, celeriac, kale, kohl rabi, turnips, swede and spinach. Make sure the last of your carrots are now out of the ground and in storage.
* Parsnips can stay in the ground, but remember you won't be able to pull them out if the ground is frozen. Jerusalem artichokes will also be ready this month.

In December, January and February you can virtually put your feet up and wait for spring when the process will start all over again. Most gardeners can't wait for the start of the warmer weather and many of my friends suffer when they can't get their regular fix in the garden. There will be just a few things you can still harvest like Brussels sprouts and parsnips, but most vegetables require the warmer months. The old cliché, 'make hay while the sun shines', is quite apt.

MAKE A COMPOST

Make sure you leave enough room in the corner of your garden for a compost heap. This will produce a wonderful, brown crumbly and sweet-smelling compost in just a few months. To get the best out of your compost you need to cover it with a tarpaulin or a piece of old carpet to help it warm up and naturally break down. After about three months, remove the compost and put it all back. This process adds air to the mixture and helps it rot even faster.

Things you can compost
* Shredded paper (as long as it is not from a glossy magazine)
* Uncooked vegetable trimmings, peelings and tea bags from your kitchen
* Annual weeds
* Old bedding plants
* Soft hedge clippings
* Dead leaves
* Lawn mowings

Things you can't compost
* Woody material like prunings
* Thick stems (must be shredded first)
* Synthetic fabrics
* Food scraps, meat or bones
* Diseased plant material
* Weeds with seedheads
* Perennial roots
* Dog or cat faeces

GREEN TOMATO CHUTNEY

This is a great way of using up all those green tomatoes that you didn't manage to ripen before the weather turned cold. This recipe should produce around 3 kg (6 lb) of chutney.

Ingredients

2.25 kg (5 lb) green tomatoes
500 g (1 lb) onions
25 g (1 oz) salt
250 g (8 oz) seedless raisins
250 g (8 oz) sultanas
1 tbsp whole black peppercorns

25 g (1 oz) root ginger
12 cloves
4 red chillies
500 g (1 lb) Demerara sugar
600 ml (1 pt) malt vinegar

Method

❋ Wash and finely chop the tomatoes. Peel and finely chop the onions. Put in a bowl and sprinkle with the salt. Leave for one hour.

❋ Transfer into a large saucepan with the raisins and sultanas. Bruise the ginger and chillies and place them in a piece of muslin with the other spices. Make sure you tie the top firmly. Add to the saucepan with the vinegar.

❋ Bring to the boil and then simmer, gradually adding the sugar until it has dissolved.

❋ Keep stirring the mixture from time to time and press into the muslin bag with the spoon to extract all the flavours. Keep cooking until the mixture has thickened.

❋ Remove the muslin bag and pour into hot sterilized jars and seal.

Planting a Herb Garden

Herbs are among the easiest things to grow in the garden and, freshly picked, will taste so much better than those dried ones you get at the supermarket. Herbs have not only been used for years in natural medicine but are also wonderful for enhancing the flavour of many recipes. Years ago I was not really aware of the damage that an excess of salt could do to your system, but today I try to use herbs instead of salt to enhance the flavour of my food.

Try to choose a spot in your garden that faces south and one that has a gentle slope to help with drainage. Start preparing your herb garden in spring and add plenty of rotted manure or compost prior to planting.

Herbs can be either evergreen, herbaceous or annual and are generally grown for their leaves or foliage. Once the herb starts to produce flowers, their leaf production slows down or stops completely, so it is important to harvest them regularly.

The evergreen herbs include sage, sosemary and thyme, and they do not die back over the winter. They will still require plenty of pruning so that you will continue to get tender, new growth. If they start to get too woody, make sure you prune them right back.

The herbaceous herbs include oregano, mint, tarragon, chives and winter savory. These plants will die back to the ground during winter, so make sure you cut them right down before the onset of winter so that they can grow back strong and healthy in the spring.

Annual herbs include coriander, basil and chervil and do not live more than one season, so you will need to plant new ones each spring. Sunlight is a major factor in growing herbs successfully and, to get the best foliage, allow plenty of space for air to circulate between each plant. Ideally the soil should be loose, not tightly packed, as the roots like plenty of room to gather the maximum amount of nutrients.

Basil – Plant consecutively over the growing season to get a constant supply.

Oregano – If you like the flavour of Italy, I would suggest at least two plants.

Chives – This herb tends to be cut and come again, so I would suggest two to three plants to keep a plentiful supply for your salads or chopped on new potatoes.

Parsley – This herb goes with most foods so plant three or four plants.

Rosemary – A very aromatic herb that is delicious with lamb or with roast potatoes. They can grow quite large so one to two plants should be sufficient.

Bay – One plant should be sufficient to give you enough leaves to flavour soups, stews and other savoury dishes.

Mint – Make sure this is planted in a container as it tends to take over the garden.

Dill – Like basil, I suggest dill is planted consecutively during the growing season.

Marjoram – You can use both the leaves and the soft seed heads for flavouring. One to two plants should be sufficient.

WHOLESOME RECIPES

Recipes from the Past

I have always been fascinated by flavours and how just one ingredient can turn an ordinary dish into an amazing recipe. Of course, the proof of the pudding is in the eating. A lot of my experience has come with experimentation and I have had quite a few disasters along the way. The best way to learn how to cook is to watch someone who knows what they are doing and ask them if they will give you a few of their secrets. Today, friends and family frequently invite themselves to dinner, so I take that as a compliment, proof that my years of sampling and trying again have paid off.

I have put together a few of the simple recipes that may have been cast aside in the modern household as more and more cookery books and television programmes try to teach you the sophisticated side to the art. These are still dishes I love to cook and ones that my children often asked for when they came home from school ravenous. To me, home cooking should be just that and, unless I am entertaining, I do not dish up food that has been built up into towers, drizzled with olive oil and then had some fancy foam deposited on the side. What I am aiming to give you with this selection of recipes is good nourishing food with the minimum of fuss – the intention is to leave people wanting more. Don't get me wrong. I am not confusing restaurant-standard food with basic cooking, I just want you to remember some of the flavours of the past.

Pea and Ham Soup

Ingredients (Serves 8)
450 g (1 lb) dry green split peas
2 litres (64 fl oz) water
1 meaty ham bone
1 onion, chopped
1 garlic clove, chopped
2 sprigs fresh marjoram
2 sprigs fresh thyme
1 stick celery, chopped
1 carrot, chopped
salt and pepper to taste

Method

* Put the dried peas in a large saucepan and cover with the water. Bring to the boil and then turn down the heat to a rolling boil for about two minutes. Take off the heat and leave to soak for at least one hour.

* Add the ham bone, chopped onion, garlic, herbs and salt and pepper. Bring the liquid back to the boil. Cover, reduce the heat and simmer for a further two hours, stirring occasionally.

* Remove any meat left on the bone and cut into small pieces. Return this meat to the pea soup with the chopped celery and carrot. Simmer the soup slowly for 45 minutes, stirring from time to time.

* Taste before serving and adjust the seasoning to your liking.

COUNTRY VEGETABLE SOUP

Ingredients (Serves 6)
  1 kg (2 lb) mixed root vegetables – carrots, celery, Jerusalem
  artichokes, leeks, onions, parsnips, potatoes, swedes, turnips
  or whatever else you have to hand
  75 g (3 oz) butter
  2 cloves garlic, sliced
  1 bay leaf
  salt and pepper to taste
  300 ml (½ pt) good chicken or vegetable stock
  a little grated cheese to garnish (optional)

Method
* Wash and prepare the vegetables by cutting them into cubes.
* Heat the butter in a large saucepan and add the vegetables,
  garlic, bay leaf and a little salt and pepper. Stir well, cover and
  cook slowly for 15 minutes, stirring occasionally.
* Add the stock, bring to the boil, then cover and simmer gently
  for 30 minutes or until the vegetables are cooked.
* Remove the bay leaf and strain the soup, reserving the liquid.
* Coarsely mash or blend half the vegetables and return to
  the liquid.
* Liquidize the remaining vegetables until they form a thick
  purée. Add to the liquid, reheat and taste for seasoning.
* If you want to add something special when serving, sprinkle
  with cheese or some herby croutons.

Farmhouse Pâté

Ingredients (Serves 6 to 8)
  350 g (¾ lb) boneless belly of pork, rinds removed and minced
  350 g (¾ lb) pig's liver, cleaned and minced
  0.25 kg (½ lb) boned pork loin, minced
  100 g (4 oz) pork fat, diced
  150 ml (¼ pt) red wine
  50 g (2 oz) can of anchovies in olive oil, drained and chopped
  1 garlic clove, crushed
  6 juniper berries, crushed
  6 black peppercorns, crushed
  1 tbsp dried mixed herbs
  8 streaky bacon rashers, rinds removed

Method
* In a large mixing bowl mix together the meats, liver and fat.
  Add the remaining ingredients, except the bacon, and stir well.
* Stretch the bacon rashers using the blade of a knife and use
  them to line the base and sides of a 1 kg (2 lb) loaf tin. Reserve
  two rashers for the top of the pâté.
* Spoon in the pâté mixture and place the two reserved rashers
  on top. Stand the tin in a *bain marie* of hot water and bake in
  a cool oven (150°C/300°F/gas mark 2) for 1½ to 2 hours, or
  until the juices are just faintly pink and the pâté has started to
  shrink away from the sides.
* When cooked, pour off the excess fat and allow to cool in the
  tin. Place a weight on a plate or greaseproof paper on top of
  the pâté to help press the meats together, then chill overnight.

WOOLTON PIE

During World War Two, Britain's Minister for Food, Lord Woolton, was keen for the nation to use its resources shrewdly, and in 1940 the Ministry issued this recipe.

Ingredients (Serves 6 to 8)
    225 g (8 oz) plain shortcrust pastry
    2 tbsp fresh sage, finely chopped
    675 g (1½ lb) mixed root vegetables such as turnip, carrot, potato, swede and leek, peeled and finely chopped
    salt and freshly ground black pepper
    6 spring onions, finely chopped
    2 onions, finely chopped
    3 tbsp fresh parsley, finely chopped
    115 g (4 oz) butter
    2 heaped tbsp plain flour
    425 ml (¾ pt) milk
    175 g (6 oz) cheddar cheese, grated (allow a little extra for sprinkling on the top)
    ½ tsp English mustard

Method
* Preheat the oven to 190°C/375°F/gas mark 5.
* Roll out the pastry on a lightly floured board which has been sprinkled with 1 tablespoon of chopped sage. Line a deep 23 cm (9 in) pie dish. Bake blind until lightly browned.
* Cook the vegetables in a pan of lightly salted, boiling water for a few minutes, or until they are just starting to soften.

Drain and return the vegetables to the pan. Add the spring onions, parsley, remaining sage and season with salt and pepper. Spoon the vegetable mixture into the pre-baked pastry case and set aside.

* Melt the butter in a saucepan, stir in the flour and cook for 1 minute, stirring to make sure the flour has cooked properly. Gradually pour in the milk, then slowly bring it to the boil, stirring constantly until the sauce thickens. Stir in the grated cheese, mustard and season to taste.

* Pour the cheese sauce over the top of the vegetables in the pastry case and sprinkle the top with some more grated cheese.

* Bake in the oven for 35 to 40 minutes, or until the top is nice and brown.

* Serve garnished with parsley and some nice new potatoes just dug up from your garden.

Chicken à la King

Ingredients (Serves 4 to 6)
1 stewing chicken, about 1.5 kg (3 lb)
1 onion, chopped
1 carrot, chopped
1 stick of celery, chopped
bouquet garni
rind and juice of 1 lemon
3 spring onions, chopped
60 g (2 oz) butter
150 g (5.5 oz) sliced mushrooms
1 green pepper, finely chopped
62 g (2 oz) flour
500 ml (16 fl oz) milk
1 teaspoon nutmeg
salt and pepper to taste
2 egg yolks
250 ml (8 fl oz) cream

Method
* Place the chicken in a large saucepan with just enough water to cover. Add the onion, carrot, celery and bouquet garni. Cover and simmer gently for 2 to 3 hours, or until the chicken is tender and starting to fall off the bone.
* When the chicken is cooked, remove the meat from the bone and dice until you have around 600 g (21 oz).
* Strain the stock through a sieve and return to the saucepan.
* Add the lemon rind and spring onions to the stock and boil

until the liquid has reduced to around 250 ml (8 fl oz). Remove the lemon rind and set aside.

* Melt the butter in a saucepan and sauté the mushrooms and pepper until soft. Stir in the flour and cook gently for a further two minutes, stirring to ensure the flour is cooked properly.

* Gradually add the milk, lemon juice and stock, and then bring to the boil, stirring continuously.

* Add the nutmeg and season with salt and pepper to taste. Add the diced chicken and cook for a further five minutes.

* Blend the egg yolks with the cream, stirring them into the chicken mixture gradually. Heat but do not allow it to come to the boil.

* Serve this dish with boiled rice and a sprig of parsley.

Sausage Casserole with Apples, Celery and Walnuts

Ingredients (Serves 4)
    454 g (16 oz) pack lean pork sausages
    1 tbsp vegetable oil
    1 onion, finely chopped
    150 g (5 oz) celery, cut into 5 cm (2 in) sticks
    250 ml (8 fl oz) cider, or 1 vegetable stock cube in 300 ml (10 fl oz) with boiling water
    2 sprigs fresh thyme, roughly chopped
    2 Bramley cooking apples, peeled, cored and quartered
    75 g (2½ oz) walnuts, halved
    3 tbsp balsamic vinegar

1 tbsp cornflour blended with 2 tbsp cold water
salt and freshly ground black pepper

Method

* Cook the sausages in a large frying pan until heated through and nicely brown. Remove from the pan and put to one side.
* Pour in the cider (or vegetable stock), add half the thyme and one of the apples. Return the sausages to the pan with the walnuts. Cover and cook on a moderate heat for about an hour.
* Blend the cornflour with a little of the balsamic vinegar. Ten minutes before the end of the cooking time, add the balsamic vinegar, cornflour mixture and the remainder of the vinegar. Increase the heat and bring to the boil, stirring constantly until the liquid thickens.
* Reduce the heat, add the remaining apple and continue to cook until the apple is soft.
* Season to taste and serve on a bed of mashed potato.

PORK AND BEANS

Ingredients (Serves 4)

1 tbsp oil
350 g (12 oz) lean belly of pork, skinned, boned and cut into narrow strips
2 onions, sliced
2 carrots, sliced
2 tsp coriander seeds, crushed
225 g (8 oz) dried red kidney beans, soaked overnight and drained

600 ml (1 pint) stock
salt and pepper

Method
* Heat the oil in a frying pan and brown the pork strips on both sides. Transfer them to a casserole.
* Add the onions to the frying pan and fry until golden brown.
* Drain off all the fat, then add the onions to the casserole with the carrots, coriander, beans, stock and season to taste with salt and pepper.
* Cover and cook in a preheated oven 160°C/325°F/gas mark 3 for 1½ to 2 hours or until the meat is very tender.
* Spoon off any excess fat and serve with your favourite potatoes and garnished with parsley.

HUNTER'S RABBIT

Ingredients (Serves 4)
1 small hard cabbage, cored and cut lengthways into pieces
25 g (1 oz) fat
450 g (1 lb) chipolata sausages
1 small onion, chopped
1 rabbit, jointed
3 to 4 bacon rashers, rinded
150 ml (¼ pt) game or chicken stock
300 ml (½ pint) dry cider
salt and pepper
bouquet garni

Method

❋ Cook the cabbage in boiling water for 5 minutes. Drain well and place in a large casserole.

❋ Melt the fat in a frying pan and fry the sausages and onion until the sausages are golden brown on all sides. Remove from the heat and drain off any fat.

❋ Place the rabbit pieces on top of the cabbage in the casserole, then add the sausages and onion. Cover with the bacon rashers. Pour in the stock and cider, and add bouquet garni. Season to taste with salt and pepper.

❋ Cover the casserole with a tight-fitting lid. Cook in a preheated oven at 150°C/300°F/gas mark 2 for 2½ hours.

COMFORTING COTTAGE PIE

Ingredients (Serves 4)
    1 tbsp oil
    1 large onion chopped
    2 medium carrots, chopped
    560 g (1¼ lb) minced beef
    400 g (14 oz) tin tomatoes
    290 ml (10 fl oz) beef stock
    1 bay leaf
    1 sprig fresh thyme
    2 tbsp tomato purée
    salt and freshly ground black pepper

For the topping
    750 g (1½ lb) potatoes, peeled and chopped

225 g (8 oz) parsnips, peeled and chopped
2 tsp creamed horseradish
75 g (2½ oz) butter
55 ml (2 fl oz) milk
grated cheese for topping

Method

* Preheat the oven to 190°C/375°F/gas mark 5.
* Heat the oil in a large saucepan. Add the onion and carrot and cook over a medium heat for 5 minutes or until soft.
* Add the minced beef and cook for a further 3 minutes until the beef is starting to brown.
* Add the tomatoes, tomato purée, beef stock, bay leaf and leaves from the thyme sprig. Cover and simmer for 30 minutes. Season to taste with salt and pepper.
* While that is cooking you can prepare the topping. Peel the potatoes and parsnips, cut into pieces and boil in water until soft. Drain and mash with the butter and milk until it is a creamy consistency. Stir in the horseradish and season with salt and pepper.
* Spoon the meat into an ovenproof dish and then top with the mash. Top with grated cheese and bake for 30 minutes until golden brown.

EVE'S PUDDING

Ingredients (Serves 6)
    450 g (1 lb) Bramley cooking apples, peeled and cored
    60 g (2 oz) Demerara (raw) sugar
    grated rind of 1 lemon
    15 ml (1 tbsp) water
    75 g (2½ oz) butter
    65 g (2 oz) caster sugar
    1 egg, beaten
    125 g (4½ oz) self-raising flour
    milk to mix

Method
* Slice the apples thinly into a greased 900 ml (1½ pt) ovenproof dish. Sprinkle the Demerara sugar and grated lemon rind over the top of the apples. Add the water.
* Cream the fat and sugar together until light and fluffy.
* Add the egg a little at a time, beating well after each addition.
* Fold in the flour with a little milk until you achieve a dropping consistency.
* Spread the cake mixture over the top of the apples. Bake in a preheated oven at 180°C/350°F/gas mark 4 for 40–45 minutes, until the apples are tender and the sponge is a light golden brown.

OLD-FASHIONED TREACLE TART

Ingredients (Serves 4 to 6)

    5 to 6 tablespoons golden syrup
    50 g (2 oz) fresh white breadcrumbs
    finely grated rind of ½ to 1 lemon
    1 tsp lemon juice
    150 g (5 oz) rich shortcrust pastry

Method

* Put the syrup into a saucepan with the breadcrumbs, lemon rind and juice and heat gently until just melted. Allow to cool.
* Roll out the pastry dough and line a 20 cm (8 in) pie dish.
* Pour in the syrup mixture.
* Using the trimmings from the pastry, roll them out and cut into long, narrow strips. Lay these strips in a trellis pattern over the top of the filling.
* Bake in a preheated oven at 200°C/400°F/gas mark 6 for 25–30 minutes or until the pastry is lightly browned.
* This tart can be served hot or cold.

CREAMY RICE PUDDING WITH APRICOT PURÉE

Ingredients (Serves 6)
   100 g (3½ oz) pudding rice
   600 ml (20 fl oz) skimmed milk
   1 tsp vanilla essence
   a pinch of ground nutmeg
   25 g (1 oz) caster sugar
   100 g (3½ oz) ready to eat dried apricots, chopped
   300 ml (10 fl oz) fresh orange juice

Method
* Place the pudding rice in a medium-sized saucepan with the milk, vanilla essence, nutmeg and caster sugar. Bring to the boil. Then reduce the heat to very low, cover and simmer for one hour, stirring occasionally. Cook until the rice is tender and the mixture looks creamy.
* While the rice is cooking, place the apricots in a small saucepan with the orange juice and simmer for 15 minutes. Allow the mixture to cool for 10 minutes and then purée in a food processor or liquidizer.
* Divide the rice pudding between six small dishes and drizzle the apricot purée over the top. Alternatively, put a layer of purée in the bottom of a glass bowl and pour the rice over the top.

THE BEST CHRISTMAS PUDDING

Ingredients (Makes 2)
  170 g (6 oz) beef suet
  2 tbsp of self-raising flour
  170 g (6 oz) soft brown sugar
  200 g (7 oz) soft, fresh white breadcrumbs
  150 g (5 oz) currants
  150 g (5 oz) raisins
  150 g (5 oz) sultanas
  110 g (4 oz) crystallized cherries chopped in half
  2 tsp mixed spice
  pinch of salt
  3 eggs
  75 ml (2.5 fl oz) of the baked flesh of a cooking apple
  zest of one large lemon
  75 ml (2.5 fl oz) of whisky

Method
* In a large bowl mix all the dry ingredients, stirring well between each addition.
* In a separate bowl beat the eggs together and add the apple purée and whisky. Stir this into the dry ingredients and mix well. Don't forget to make a wish at this stage.
* Grease a couple of 1½ pint pudding basins and divide the mixture between them. Cover the top with greaseproof paper and tie it securely under the rim of the basin.
* Steam the puddings for about 8–9 hours in a large saucepan, making sure that the water level remains halfway up the bowl. Make sure that you do not allow the water to boil dry

or that it boils over the top of the bowl. Check the water level every hour and top up if necessary with boiling water.

* Store this long-lasting pudding in a cool, dry place and steam for another couple of hours before you want to eat it.

GINGER PUDDING

Ingredients (Serves 6)
200 g (7 oz) plain flour
2 tsp ground ginger
a pinch of salt
1 tsp bicarbonate of soda
100 g (3½ oz) shredded suet
65 g (2 oz) caster sugar
1 tbsp black treacle
1 egg
75–100 ml (2.5–3.5 fl oz) milk
fat for greasing

Method
* Sift the flour, ginger, bicarbonate of soda and salt into a bowl. Add the suet and sugar.
* Beat the treacle and egg together with about 50 ml (1.8 fl oz) milk. Stir this into the dry ingredients, adding more milk if necessary to give a soft dropping consistency.
* Put into a greased 1 litre pudding basic, cover with greaseproof paper and steam for 1½ to 2 hours. Delicious served with golden syrup and custard.

Chocolate Cherry Brownies

Ingredients (Makes 12 brownies)

175 g (6 oz) self-raising white flour
50 g (1¾ oz) cocoa powder
100 g (3½ oz) soft dark brown sugar
100 g (3½ oz) butter, melted
1 egg
175 ml (6 fl oz) skimmed milk
1 tsp almond essence
150 g (5½ oz) canned cherries, drained and stoned
25 g (1 oz) milk chocolate chips

Method

* Preheat the oven to gas mark 180°C/350°F/gas mark 4. Line a 20 cm (8 in) square tin with non-stick baking parchment.
* Sift the flour and cocoa powder together in a mixing bowl and then mix in the sugar.
* Pour the butter over the dry ingredients along with the egg, milk and almond essence, and mix until it forms a soft batter. Fold in the cherries and chocolate chips.
* Pour the mixture into the prepared tins and bake for 25 minutes.
* Leave it to cool in the tin for 15 minutes and then carefully transfer it to a wire rack to cool completely. Do not attempt to cut it while it is still warm. Cut into 12 slices.

Fruited Bran Loaf

Ingredients (Makes 1 loaf)
  55 g (2 oz) bran
  135 g (4¾ oz) brown sugar
  225 g (8 oz) dried fruit
  250 ml (8 fl oz) milk
  175 g (6 oz) self-raising flour

Method
* Preheat the oven to 180°C/350°F/gas mark 4.
* Put the bran, sugar and dried fruit into a bowl and mix thoroughly.
* Stir in the milk. Add the flour and mix well.
* Pour the mixture into a well-greased 450 g (1 lb) loaf tin and bake for 1¼ hours or until a cake tester comes out clean.
* Turn out on to a wire rack and leave to cool.
* Serve sliced with lashings of butter.

Crusty Bread Rolls

Ingredients (Makes 12 rolls)
  15 g (½ oz) fresh yeast
  250–300 ml (9–10 fl oz) tepid milk
  1 tsp caster sugar
  450 g (1 lb) strong plain flour
  1 tsp salt
  50 g (2 oz) butter

Method

❋ Blend the yeast with 150 ml (5 fl oz) of the milk and sugar.

❋ Sift flour and salt, add the butter, and rub into the flour until it resembles fine breadcrumbs.

❋ Stir in the yeast mixture and enough milk to make a fairly soft dough.

❋ Turn the dough on to a floured surface and knead thoroughly for 10 minutes or until the dough is firm, elastic and no longer sticky. Place in a large bowl, cover with a clean tea towel and leave to rise in a warm place until it has doubled in size. This should take between 1 and 2 hours.

❋ Turn on to a floured surface and knead well for 2 to 3 minutes. Divide into 12 equal pieces and shape into rolls.

❋ Place the rolls on greased baking sheets, leaving plenty of space for them to spread. Cover with the tea towel and leave to prove until they have doubled in size. Cut slits in the top of each roll.

❋ Bake in a preheated oven at 230°C/450°F/gas mark 8 for 15–20 minutes or until well risen and golden.

❋ As a finishing touch, you can sprinkle your rolls with poppy seeds or any other topping of your choice before baking.

RHUBARB AND GINGER JAM

Ingredients (Makes 1.4 kg/3 lb)
  1.1 kg (2½ lb) trimmed rhubarb, chopped
  1.1 kg (2½ lb) sugar
  juice of 2 lemons
  25 g (1 oz) fresh root ginger
  100 g (4 oz) preserved or crystallized ginger, chopped

Method
* Put the rhubarb in a large bowl in alternate layers with the sugar and lemon juice. Cover the bowl and leave overnight.
* The following day, bruise the ginger with a rolling pin and then tie it in a piece of muslin. Put the rhubarb mixture into a preserving pan with the muslin bag and bring to the boil. Boil rapidly for 15 minutes.
* Remove the muslin bag, add the preserved or crystallized ginger and boil for a further 5 minutes or until the rhubarb is clear. Test to see if it is at setting point.
* When setting point is reached, take the pan off the heat and skim the surface with a slotted spoon.
* Pour the jam into warm, sterilized jars and seal with lids.

HOW TO TEST FOR SETTING POINT

To test for setting point, drip a little of the jam on to a cold plate. Allow to cool for 2 to 3 minutes and, if the surface wrinkles when pushed gently with the finger, the jam is ready for bottling.

Strawberry Jam

Ingredients (Makes 1.4 kg/3 lb)
  1 kg (2 lb) of strawberries
  buttered paper
  675g (1½lb) granulated sugar
  juice of one lemon, strained
  1 tsp brandy or sherry

Method

* Remove the husks from the strawberries. Butter the inside of a preserving pan very lightly with buttered paper to reduce the scum.
* Place a single layer of strawberries in the pan and cover with a layer of sugar. Continue layering the fruit and sugar, cover, and leave overnight. By the next morning the sugar will have nearly all dissolved and the juice will have separated from the fruit.
* Place the pan over a medium to low heat and leave until the remaining sugar has completely dissolved. Shake the pan occasionally but do not stir.
* After 30 minutes, increase the heat to medium high and add the strained lemon juice. Shake the pan to distribute it and, when boiling, cook for exactly 8 minutes.
* Test for setting point. If it has not reached the right point then continue boiling for another 3 minutes.
* Pour the jam into heated jars, cover the surface with a disc of waxed paper dipped in brandy or sherry to seal. Finally put the lids on and enjoy with some scones and cream.

INDEX

Note: Headings in *italic* refer to recipes